The Pursuit
of Truth

THE PURSUIT OF TRUTH

A Historian's Memoir

WILLIAM H. McNEILL

THE UNIVERSITY PRESS OF KENTUCKY

Publication of this volume was made possible in part by a grant
from the National Endowment for the Humanities.

Scholarly publisher for the Commonwealth,
serving Bellarmine University, Berea College, Centre College of Kentucky, Eastern Kentucky
University, The Filson Historical Society, Georgetown College, Kentucky Historical Society,
Kentucky State University, Morehead State University, Murray State University,
Northern Kentucky University, Transylvania University, University of Kentucky,
University of Louisville, and Western Kentucky University.

Cover/Frontispiece Photo: Courtesy of Harvard University Press

Editorial and Sales Offices: The University Press of Kentucky
663 South Limestone Street, Lexington, Kentucky 40508-4008
www.kentuckypress.com

05 06 07 08 09   5 4 3 2 1

Library of Congress Cataloging-in-Publication Data

McNeill, William Hardy, 1917-
The pursuit of truth : a historian's memoir / William H. McNeill.
    p. cm.
Includes index.
ISBN 0-8131-2345-3 (hardcover : alk. paper)
1. McNeill, William Hardy, 1917- 2. Historians—Canada—Biography. I. Title.
D15.M38A3 2005
907'.2'02—dc22   2004024345

Manufactured in the United States of America.

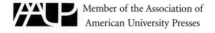

Member of the Association of
American University Presses

Contents

Illustrations follow page 88

Preface

This memoir has been slow to achieve its present form. When my children read an earlier version they advised against publication on the ground that it was too narrowly personal and of no general interest. I then set out to broaden its scope by acknowledging indebtedness to others, thus connecting myself with intellectual developments in my lifetime more adequately than before.

Then, in January 2003, before I had even started on that revision, Stephen Wrinn of the University Press of Kentucky invited me to write "a brief manuscript about the changes in the historical profession" that had occurred during my career. I responded by saying that I was thinking of a more personal memoir that would focus on how world history fared, rather than on changes in the historical profession at large, but that would address general issues too. In particular, I aimed at rebutting the prejudice that makes world history unacceptable to most historians because no one can assure accuracy by writing about the whole world using primary sources in all the original languages.

I remain unrepentant, claiming that inferences and large doses of imagination actually have allowed the construction of a far more adequate understanding of the cosmic and human past than earlier generations achieved. I even believe that this is the central intellectual accomplishment of the twentieth century. Innumerable cosmologists, physicists, mathematicians, anthropologists, sociologists, historians, ecologists, ethologists, and other specialists played their part; a few swashbuckling intellects led the way, and the outlines of an evolutionary worldview, uniting natural and human history, has begun to emerge. It may be convincing for generations to come—or again may not.

My personal role was confined to the human segment of this past, and I was only one among many. Successors will discover defects in what seems persuasive today; but no one can deny that information and understanding about the history of humankind as a whole enlarged their scope and precision enormously across the past six decades. Recording one person's part in that effort and portraying some of the encounters that shaped my ideas is a partial, subjective version of what transpired. But if the emerging evolutionary worldview, fitting humanity firmly into an evolving ecological and natural setting, proves enduringly attractive, this sort of personal testimony from a participant may justify publication despite, or even because of, the idiosyncratic, biased story it has to tell.

CHAPTER 1

From Childhood to World War II
1917–1941

I was born on 31 October 1917 in Vancouver, British Columbia, Canada. That day happened to be the four hundredth anniversary of the beginning of the Protestant Reformation in Germany, and my father, who was then teaching church history at a newly established Presbyterian college in Westminster, B.C., noted that fact with some satisfaction. Later in life I was more impressed by the fact that my birth occurred a week before Lenin inaugurated the Bolshevik Revolution in Russia—a different, and more fleeting, historical landmark.

These coincidences did not make me into a historian. Instead it was my father's example. He was a medievalist by training and took the history of the Christian church in western Europe as his bailiwick, teaching courses and writing books that spanned the centuries from Constantine's time to the twentieth century. He had encountered an ecumenical version of church history in 1912–13 at Edinburgh, where he won a year's scholarship, and became convinced that what united quarreling Protestant sects was more important than the theological wrangles that divided them. Thereafter he sought to turn church history into an exploration of the commonalities that bound Christians together, instead of using it to show how a particular denomination had preserved the true faith, while everyone else had fallen away from it across the centuries, as church historians had done ever since the Reformation.

An irenic, transdenominational version of church history was novel, even radical, in 1912. It became my father's life work to propagate such a vision of the Christian past, and I eventually came to recognize how closely my own career as a world historian replicated that of my father. For I, in my time, set out to look across civilizational, just as he had looked across sectarian, boundaries. But it took me a long while to live down youthful differences with him, in matters intellectual as well as personal. This memoir, in effect, is an effort to achieve an appropriately balanced appraisal of his and other influences that combined to shape my understanding of history in particular and the world in general.

My father was a farm boy from Prince Edward Island in Canada who, having excelled in school, went on to college and then became a Presbyterian minister. He combined theological training with graduate study, first at McGill University, where he earned an M.A. in English, then at the University of Chicago, where he got a Ph.D. in history in 1920. My mother's career was rather more exceptional. She was born in Vancouver Island at the opposite extreme of Canada and was of Scottish descent, yet also went to McGill and, like my father, emerged as valedictorian of her class. At that time in Canada it was most unusual for a woman to attend college, especially coming, as she did, from raw frontier society in British Columbia, where higher education was an exotic irrelevance in nearly everyone's eyes. But a favorite teacher, who had gone to college herself in Nova Scotia,

urged my mother to pursue a college degree. With this encourage-
ment, Netta Hardy's ambition flamed so high that it carried her
across the continent to attend McGill, since no college in British Columbia then offered a B.A. A wealthy uncle funded her adventure.
This distressed her parents, who felt that, as their eldest child, she
should stay home and help to raise her eight younger siblings until
such time as marriage took her away.

My birth came only nine and a half months after her marriage,
and this both embarrassed and pleased my mother. Above all, it
meant that she was rapturously received into the McNeill family by
my father's parents in Prince Edward Island, simply for having given
birth to a son who would carry on the name. I gave her, in effect, a
new family to belong to, and one that respected, even reverenced,
higher education. For my McNeill grandparents sympathized with
and admired my father's career, even though it meant that their only
surviving son would not be available to help with farm work and
succeed to the family farm as my grandfather aged.

For my mother, therefore, I was not only her eldest and only son
but a ticket to a new and welcoming family identity. Consequently,
I became the apple of her eye, and in later years she often invited
me to substitute for my father by doing household chores that he
was too busy to attend to. She also followed my career in high school
and college more avidly than anyone else, and in general kept me
close-tied to her apron strings until I belatedly left home in 1939 to
start Ph.D. work at Cornell. I thus remained Mother's Boy far longer
than usual, and reciprocated her affection. I still suppose that I inherited a reckless, roving cast of mind largely from her. My father's
linguistic skills were much superior to my own; and his style of
scholarship was more careful, minute, and, above all, far more text-
bound than my hasty and speculative bent. My mother's mind was

also bold and imaginative—or so it seemed to me when I was still at home, wrestling with new ideas. Perhaps that only means that she listened attentively even to callow and dogmatic remarks that I sometimes flung at her during my adolescent years. Later in life, she changed and became conspicuously pious, even timorous; but when I knew her best she seemed a fellow spirit, receptive to many of my half-baked notions.

She taught me to read at home before I started kindergarten. I cooperated largely to keep ahead of my sister Isabel, thirteen months younger than myself, whose prowess in her early schooling far excelled mine. Nonetheless, I too became a reader, and before the age of ten, when we migrated from Toronto to Chicago, I had read all but one of Walter Scott's Waverley novels as well as a good many other full-length books. My parents read aloud to us every night at bedtime for an hour or more, mixing novels and poems with hymns and excerpts from the Bible. Scottish history and literature figured prominently in what they read to us, supplemented by some distinctly patriotic Canadian texts.

Sunday school offered little intellectual stimulus; but I also attended adult services at Bloor Street Presbyterian Church in Toronto between 1922 and 1927, where I had the privilege of listening to the Reverend George Pidgeon. He was an impressive figure, broad shouldered, deep voiced and more than six feet tall. More importantly, he was perfectly assured of his version of Christian truth and spelled it out each Sunday in logically precise, carefully organized commentaries on the biblical texts he had chosen for the day. Sometimes when we were sitting at dinner afterward, my father asked me to summarize the sermon. I can still remember how George Pidgeon's logic and rhetoric made that easy to do, for he began by announcing three or four points he was going to make, then explained each of them, and

4

summarized the lesson again at the close. His sermons were, in fact, a model of intellectual discourse—clear, elegant, exact, and serenely eloquent as well.

Overall, as a small boy, I was well and truly soaked in words of the English language, and found no difficulty in spouting them back. Mind you, exactitude was never my forte. I was an indifferent speller, having early learned to read about half a line of type at a glance. This made for speed but also meant that I never looked at a given word in detail, and if I got it wrong when first it entered my vocabulary, it stayed that way. Thus even when I was in college, I used the spelling "seperate," as the word is pronounced, and on one occasion barely restrained myself from correcting Professor Richard McKeon when he wrote "separate" on the blackboard.

Instead, from the very beginning I looked for large-scale patterns. For example, when walking with my father to his office at the University of Toronto, I once tried out on him an idea I had just hatched, to wit, that the medieval kingdoms of England and Scotland lagged behind the kingdom of France because their respective founders, King Alfred, King David, and Charlemagne, reigned approximately a century apart. Instead of agreeing with me, as I had hoped, my father neither contradicted nor endorsed my bright idea. Doubtless he saw its absurdity, for Charlemagne was a German, so did not, in any meaningful sense, found the French monarchy, and in view of subsequent Danish and Norman conquests, King Alfred's claim to be founder of the English monarchy was more a figment of nineteenth-century Anglo-Saxon piety than historical fact. My father refrained from saying so but also disappointed me by not accepting my idea. If he had told me why I was wrong, I wonder how I would have reacted? I like to think that I might have been able to accept correction—but he did not put me to the test, being perhaps preoccupied with his own thoughts or afraid of discouraging my childish enthusiasm.

This was, all the same, the first original historical idea I ever entertained, so far as I can tell. I was obviously trying to put things together and find a common pattern across separate national histories as concocted by patriotic nineteenth-century historians, and transmitted to me mostly by bedtime reading. (I can remember, for instance, persuading my father to read to us *A Short History of Scotland* by a professor named Brown—a narrowly political account of absolutely no interest to my two sisters.) It seems mildly surprising, all the same, to recognize that my lifelong attraction to simple ideas, bridging separate domains of discourse, manifested itself before I was ten years old. For a long time I assumed that everyone else was fascinated by large views and as eager to understand the whole wide world as I was. Indeed I still feel they ought to be!

Schoolwork came easily to me on the whole, but I remember little in the way of intellectual stimulus. When in 1927 we moved to Chicago, I brought with me from the Huron Street Public School in Toronto a far better knowledge of geography than existed among pupils of the University of Chicago Laboratory School, and I was clearly ahead of my age group in such subjects as math. But I liked the young and pretty fifth-grade teacher, Ida DePencier, to whom I was first assigned. A few weeks later I was promoted to sixth grade where I belonged in terms of the general level of classroom work. But I promptly recoiled from my new teacher and soon persuaded the authorities to return me to the easy environs existing among my age-mates in fifth grade.

I coasted through school for the next few years, without difficulty and without enthusiasm. The main thing I remember having learned was how to make an outline before writing a paper. This was prescribed by the "unit system of learning" that then prevailed in the Lab School, and which had been unknown in Toronto. I therefore encountered it in Mrs. DePencier's class for the first time. I still remember delighting in the simplicity and logical completeness of her scheme when she began outlining a unit we had just completed on the fall of the Roman Empire by writing two Roman numeraled primary headings on the blackboard, "Internal Causes" and "External Causes," and then proceeded to solicit from us subordinate entries, *A*, *B*, *C*, etc., under each of these heads.

Later in life, the habit of making an outline ahead of time served me well when I started to write essays and books. Long after she had retired, I once had occasion to mention my indebtedness to her, and she told me that making an outline was something she had always dreaded and never felt secure in doing in front of her pupils. Maybe so: certainly the scheme she offered and that I embraced so warmly was not in itself particularly insightful. But the effort to see the whole and its parts from beginning to end by outlining a subject before one writes was, I still think, the principal skill the Lab School imparted to me.

I actually remember only two moments when a sudden new insight dawned on me in class. One was in math, in my junior year in high school, when a teacher named Mr. Stone was discussing an algebraic problem and his words and the symbols he put on the blackboard somehow precipitated a sudden illumination. But I cannot reconstruct the exact nature of the problem; I only remember an instantaneous flash of understanding and the warm sense of satisfaction that accompanied it. A second such moment came early in my college years when President Hutchins and Mortimer Adler provoked a similar leap of understanding by asking questions about Plato's *Republic*. This time I put up my hand and explained a newly glimpsed congruence that I had recognized between two seemingly discordant passages, and did so to their satisfaction and my own. But again details elude me now. I only recall the exhilaration of instantaneous discovery, connecting what had been separate and recognizing harmony where apparent contradiction had prevailed.

Most similar sudden insights and imaginative leaps came privately, as a by-product of more and more strenuous study and my desire to do well in school. Classroom work first engaged real enthusiasm during my sophomore year in high school when I took a course in ancient and medieval history from Mr. Barnard. We used a purple-bound textbook he had written, and he habitually started each class by repeating matter from it, then weaving in errors and becoming more and more recklessly inventive until someone recognized what he was doing and corrected him. It was a game that certainly got my attention, and the one-page papers he required at the conclusion of each unit of study were the first such efforts that really challenged me as I set out to select and organize what mattered most and squeeze it all into the brief compass we were allowed. From that time I began to sublimate dawning sexual impulses by excelling in schoolwork, so by the time we graduated, I ranked second in the senior class.

I departed from parental paths significantly and abruptly one Sunday morning when, sitting in the family pew of the Hyde Park United Church and idly twisting a loose button on the cushion beside me, I said to myself, "I do not believe in God." Some months previously I had attended a confirmation class. But when our minister, Douglas Horton, fell back on St. Anselm's (d. 1109) ontological argument[1] to prove the existence of God, he entirely failed to convince me. Quite the contrary, the argument struck me as an abuse of language. Though I duly submitted to the ritual of confirmation, and never discussed Christian belief with my parents or anyone else, Douglas Horton's unconvincing argument had sown doubt in my mind; and for no reason I can assign, on that morning, listening to his more emotional, hortatory rhetoric instead of to the calm certainty that had prevailed in George Pidgeon's Toronto pulpit, the balance tipped, committing me to secret, personal rejection of the Christian piety my parents held dear. This occurred when I was still in high school—probably in 1932—and in a true sense signified the beginning of my effort to understand the world on my own, independently of parents, teachers, and ecclesiastical authority or tradition.

In saying to myself, "I do not believe in God," I was rejecting the notion that a person, or anything like a human person, was in charge of the universe. All of a sudden, that idea became preposterous to me. The mere scale of the starry firmament, the minuteness of earth, and the slender scum of life that cluttered its surface made it impossible for me to suppose that the human species had been created in the image of God. Rather, men had created the Christian God in their own image, projecting an imaginary, stern yet (sometimes) loving Father upon the universe. How absurd; how threatening; how (sometimes) comforting! But in the pride of my youth, and throughout my adult years, being privileged to lead an easy, comfortable life, I did not need religious faith, threat, or comfort, so I never altered my youthful skepticism.

At almost the same time, in 1933–34, I took a full-blown college course on the University of Chicago campus. This was part of an experiment by President Hutchins to see whether combining the last two years of high school with the first two years of college might make a more rigorous curriculum possible for what he called "General Education." This he hoped might provide a rational, philosophical guide to adult life and citizenship, replacing the vanished religious certainties he had grown up to reject—and regret. Ironically, a scheme of general education, principally embodied in four survey courses introduced at Chicago immediately after Hutchins took office in 1930, had been shaped by others who did not share his philosophical quest; and this was what I encountered when Hutchins began to tinker with prevailing patterns and someone (perhaps the high school principal) decided that the humanities survey would be the most suitable college course for high school seniors to take. I was among the chosen few, and for nine months—October to June—I sat anonymously with hundreds of others in Mandel Hall, listening to three lectures a week and attending a discussion section on Mondays, led by a graduate student from the History Department named Eugene Anderson.

The architect and principal lecturer in the humanities course was an elderly history professor named Ferdinand Schevill. Shaped by German scholarship and an occasional practitioner of *Geistesgeschichte* in his own right, Schevill made the introductory course in the humanities into a History of Western Civilization by exposing raw freshmen to selections from European literature, art, and music conceived of as expressing the spirit of successive ages.

Week after week, readings and other experiences incidental to that course had revelatory force for me, since I had been strictly raised within a rather narrow canon of Scottish Presbyterian propriety. For example, I learned the Christian doctrines of sin, grace, and redemption by eating the body of God, the Christ, only when I read Anselm's *Cur Deus Homo*—an almost incredible proof of how energetically my parents and the ministers I had listened to shrank from that awkward doctrine. Similarly, Flaubert's novel *Madame Bovary* brought the possibility of marital infidelity to my attention for the first time. I likewise remember (and shared) the intense embarrassment Eugene Anderson radiated when he carried a reproduction of Matisse's *Dance* (1909), featuring a circle of distorted, naked women, into the classroom and invited us to discuss it. Two other moments lodge in my memory: a lecture on the life and death of Socrates by a youthful teacher of philosophy named Osborne, and a parallel lecture he gave on the life and death of Jesus. He treated them both as admirable and influential human beings—an approach both new and attractive to me.

Later in life, when I was collaborating on the task of designing a different course in the History of Western Civilization at Chicago, I realized that Schevill's course was constructed around a dichotomy between faith and reason, pagan Greece and Christian Rome, Saint Socrates and Saint Paul. That was the cultural heritage he set out to explore with us, and his sympathies and those of almost all of our other teachers were wholly on the secular side. I had already been exposed in my junior year of high school to Carl Becker's even more rigorously secular vision of modern European history in the form of his then brand-new textbook. Becker celebrated the French style of Enlightenment and its transfer to American shores as the central event of the modern age, and conveniently disposed of religion by deleting it from the historical record in subsequent times. What Schevill's humanities course did, in effect, was to extend a similar secular, rationalistic version of the European past across ancient and medieval history, and by doing so, it opened spacious new horizons before me. I took no notes on the lectures, readings, and discussions of the humanities course, probably because no one told me to; but it all came home to me so vividly that when I took the comprehensive examination I got an A.

The experience of that course convinced me that the University of Chicago was the place for me to pursue truth and enlarge my understanding of the world. Since staying home was cheaper than paying for room and board elsewhere and, partly for that reason, conformed to my parents' preferences, the matter was simply taken for granted. When the time to register for the 1934–35 school year came round, I therefore showed up at Bartlett Gym with my high school diploma in hand and was accepted as a student without any of the admissions procedures that became mandatory afterward. But the Depression was then acute, and every additional student meant a hundred dollars' extra tuition per quarter—a sum which was relatively easy for me and my parents to afford. It was, altogether, a much simpler age than what faced my children a generation later.

My college years, 1934–38, were intensely stimulating. At the time I was convinced that a Chicago undergraduate education was the best in the country, and I have never changed my mind, even though defects in the four survey courses—Humanities, Social Science, Biological Science, and Physical Science—and the limitations of more specialized courses in history and other subjects that dominated the last two years of my undergraduate experience now seem obvious. But given the blank page I brought to most of my courses, and a growing skill at rapid assimilation of whatever was put in front of me, almost every course and every teacher was an eye-opener and delight. My grades reflected my enthusiasm—and more than a whiff of pride as well. (Once, for example, a C on a phy sci quiz so offended me that I undertook a review of everything we had studied to date, and duly emerged in June with an A for the course as a whole.) In my senior year I was appointed Student Head Marshal—a dignity recognizing both curricular and extracurricular distinction. In effect, I therefore matched my parents' feats of becoming valedictorians of their respective classes at McGill, though at Chicago the Student Head Marshal made no speeches and came away with a silver-headed baton instead of a parchment certificate.

Each of the four required survey courses was a revelation to me, though all were something of an anticlimax to the baptismal Humanities History of Western Civilization. I came away from the two science surveys superficially acquainted with what was already a rather old-fashioned version of contemporary natural science. Relativity and quantum mechanics were mentioned, for example, but not explained; the stars were still eternal; and both subatomic particles and biochemistry were discreetly omitted. But that scarcely mattered. The two courses persuaded me that, in some sense, I understood the natural world. The illusion endured, for later in life, as new developments revolutionized astronomy, physics, and biology, I tagged along by reading popular accounts, believing that the natural world out there was somehow within my reach, even without the mathematics that made quantum mechanics so mysteriously plausible.

More important for me was the social science survey. This was then presided over by Harry Gideonse, a young economist who fancied himself as Hutchins's most articulate faculty opponent. The course itself made no pretense of integrating the social sciences. Instead it devoted successive quarters to introductory economics, sociology, and political science. The economics of marginal utility and political science embodied in American forms of government left me cold; but the winter quarter of sociology did bring a pair of ideas to my attention that I have clung to ever since. One came from reading an excerpt from William Graham Sumner's *Folkways*, to wit, the notion that use and wont are stubborn even, or especially, when irrational; and that the texture of everyday life is largely governed by such routinized behavior. The second springs from John Dewey's

13

Human Nature and Conduct, which, if I remember rightly, we read all the way through. What stuck to me from Dewey's pages was the related idea that abstract human thought is a reaction to frustrated habit—what people often (but not always) do when the outcome of their action disappoints their expectation. I concluded that unthinking, habitual action is the natural and truly happy way of life; whereas thought is a symptom of dysfunction but conducive to survival all the same since, every so often, new thoughts find ways of escaping the frustration that provoked them by inventing satisfying new ways to get things done.

In all probability, what I remember about both these books distorts what they have to say. But communication always involves slippage, and intellectual discourse is particularly liable to being twisted since a recipient can only accommodate novelty by fitting it into a preexisting structure of ideas. I was busily doing so throughout my undergraduate years, greedily snatching at new notions and trying to fit them into a tangle of ideas already cluttering my mind.

Formal classes, of course, were only part of my undergraduate experience and in some ways were less significant than extracurricular encounters with fellow students. For example, at the time I arrived on campus in 1934, Marxism was a missionary faith among a handful of students, who were, however, divided into three rival, disputatious sects—reformist Socialists, revolutionary Communists, and even more revolutionary Trotskyites. Communists could boast the achievements of the first and second Five-year Plans in Russia at a time when persistent depression prevailed in the U.S. and the rest of the capitalist world. But there were doubts. Trotskyites, in particular, denounced Stalin's heresies, and the spectacular treason trials of 1936–38 soon showed that all was not well within the Soviet Union. The social science survey course also contributed to my introduction to Marxism by requiring me to read the *Communist Manifesto*, and I was much impressed by the schematic version of the past and future of humanity that Marx sketched in that document. But I never became a Marxist, held back mainly by the dogmatism and, above all, by the discipline of submitting to a party line that prevailed among all varieties of student Marxists. Instead I clung to my own presumptuous quest for a personal version of truth and righteousness.

Marxism affected most American campuses in the 1930s, but Chicago was unique in becoming the seat of a rival missionary faith, also divided into discordant sects. Richard McKeon, professor of philosophy and, ere long, also dean of the Humanities Division, attracted a very considerable following for his version of Aristotelianism. Simultaneously, Mortimer Adler, another philosopher, precariously lodged in the Law School, promulgated his own rather more flamboyant form of Aristotelian Thomism,[2] while President Hutchins presided over the resultant philosophical rumpus, pursuing his own heartfelt search for rational truth (or truths?), which, I believe, he never actually found.

Throughout my undergraduate years he and Adler co-taught an evening class that went by the title "Classics of the Western World." I attended its meetings for two years, in the course of which we went through Plato's *Republic* as translated by Benjamin Jowett almost line by line, then read Genesis and some other passages from the King James Bible. That was about all we discussed in two whole years. Neither Adler nor Hutchins knew Greek, and I have since wondered how drastically their discourse and my own struggles with philosophical questions were governed by the translations we used. McKeon did know Greek, but his own personal philosophy, purporting to embrace all intellectual discourse by fitting it into either an Aristotelian or a Platonic mold, rode roughshod over textual details, and eventually I concluded that he was clever but not wise and was sometimes intellectually irresponsible as well.

I reached that conclusion when, as an M.A. candidate in 1939, I took a course in Hellenistic philosophy from him. One day, having written three terms on the blackboard, he asserted that "oddly enough" each of three philosophers made one of those terms fundamental while treating the other two as derivative. A certain hesitancy in his voice when he named the third of these philosophers made me suspicious, and by then I knew enough to think of checking up on McKeon by looking in Pauly-Wissowa, an authoritative, encyclopedic compilation of information about Greek and Roman writers and their texts. Sure enough the appropriate entry was very brief, declaring that nothing was known but the name of this particular philosopher. McKeon, I concluded, needed another name to complete his scheme, so took this one from thin air—or perhaps from Pauly-Wissowa. I never mentioned the matter to him or to anyone else, but from that time onward my respect for him largely evaporated.

My reaction to Adler and Hutchins was different. Adler struck me as far too nimble at winning arguments to be really convincing. But I did admire Hutchins and, perhaps mistakenly, projected onto him my own concern for, and inability to find, satisfactory answers to Plato's questions about knowledge, truth, beauty, and good. Accordingly, the two years I spent in their class were central to my personal wrestling matches with philosophical questions. Most of the time I was silent as was my wont in all my classes; but on one occasion I burst out in protest against how, at the close of Book I of *The Republic* (Sections 336–54), Plato seemed satisfied with the flimsy wordplay Socrates used to rebut Thrasymachus's claim that justice was no more than the interest of the stronger. I do not remember what followed, but feel pretty sure that no one convinced me that Socrates' refutation was logically adequate or fair. Years later one of my friends asked me whether I still believed that Thrasymachus was right. I had forgotten all about it by then and had no answer—but it shows that I was not alone in my intense engagement with epistemological and moral questions.

Two extracurricular settings became central to my life as an undergraduate. One was the Beta Theta Pi fraternity. I joined it sometime in 1935. The Chicago chapter had been on the verge of collapse when Norman Maclean, then an instructor in the humanities course from the English Department, and himself a Beta, persuaded members of an extracurricular discussion group he had organized to take over the fraternity house and find enough like-minded recruits to continue their discussions indefinitely into the future. Such a spirit, and the collection of high-achievers Maclean's campaign attracted, made for a most unusual fraternity—so much so that in my senior year every graduating Beta at Chicago qualified for Phi Beta Kappa.

In the meanwhile occasional meals at the fraternity house and weekly chapter meetings brought me into contact with a variety of enthusiasts among whom the winds of doctrine sweeping the campus achieved extraordinary intensity. I watched, for example, how an unusually articulate poet and Marxist transformed himself into a Thomist and eventually became a Dominican friar. Others became disciples of McKeon; still others developed a cult of Mozart, whose birthday we all celebrated with a special dinner followed by recordings of his music. Living at home, I always remained marginal, yet I made some good friends, shared in endless talk, and deliberately cultivated the art of conversation with prospective Beta members during the annual fraternity rush. After chapter meetings, when walking home with one or another of my home-dwelling fraternity brothers, we frequently prolonged an argument late into the night standing on a street corner where our paths diverged.

My attachment to the group of students who published the *Daily Maroon* was considerably stronger, since on four afternoons a week, when a paper was due to appear the next day, I showed up in the *Maroon* office to do whatever might be assigned to me. Beginners ran errands and hung around doing odd jobs. As sophomores we were assigned to regular beats around campus and were expected to ferret out news and then write it up and submit our stories to the managing editor, a senior, who either accepted it, rejected it, or asked for a rewrite. Newspaper work was not entirely new to me since I had edited a weekly four-page paper in high school; but that experience had lasted only a year, and I never put much effort into it. The *Maroon*, however, gradually became the center of my extracurricular life, and when walking home at the end of the day, I felt content whenever I had an article coming out on the morrow and was correspondingly disappointed when I did not. Gradually I became so addicted to print that I still feel that a day when I have not written something destined for publication is irremediably second best.

In my junior year, in addition to daytime reporting I became a night editor, responsible for putting the paper to bed about once every two weeks. This required going to a print shop near the corner of Cottage Grove Avenue and 63rd Street, a most unsavory neighborhood, and staying there until two or three in the morning. By that time, linotype operators had set stories, ads, and headlines; the night editor had proofread everything; and six to eight pages of type, pictures, and ads had been locked into forms that, when run through the flat bed press, would create the next day's paper. One lino-type operator—a clever and not unkindly woman—liked to invent witty or obscene typos to test our proofreading—a game I played with more anxiety than joy. But extended contact with the unionized workers in that shop was my first and only significant exposure to industrial America, and I count it as a valuable part of my education. I also realize in retrospect how much my late hours must have worried my parents who knew full well that walking those streets late at night was an invitation to armed robbery. Nothing of the kind ever happened to me, but I was always aware of risk going home from across the Midway—a walk of about a mile.

In my senior year I became editor-in-chief, fulfilling an ambition far more intense than any I have since felt. Appointment depended on choices made by six seniors who constituted the paper's Board of Control, and I still do not know why the retiring editor, a fraternity brother of my principal rival, ElRoy Golding, did not choose him. Traditionally, fraternity affiliation had often been decisive for attaining leadership of extracurricular organizations; but in this case my hopes were realized and ElRoy became a somewhat disgruntled managing editor on the Board of Control over which I presided during the school year 1937–38.

By long-standing convention, the editor-in-chief wrote editorials of between five hundred and six hundred words four times a week. My predecessors often struggled to find something to say, but I never ran out of words and learned to write editorials at top speed each afternoon amidst the hubbub of the *Maroon* office and despite frequent interruptions. I began the year by laying down a five-point platform for University of Chicago reform, of which the most controversial were "The abolition of Inter-collegiate athletics" and "A chastened President."

Chicago had been a pioneer in big-time college athletics and won its last Big Ten football championship in 1927. But anonymously graded comprehensive exams for each of the required survey courses, instituted in 1930, made it impossible for athletes to continue retaining their eligibility by taking "gut" courses from professors whose grades reflected their own enthusiasm for sports rather than academic accomplishment. The result was that Chicago's teams became uncompetitive in the Big Ten, and the resulting humiliation—I had been an enthusiastic follower of Chicago football and basketball in my early student years—damaged the university's public image. Or so I thought. Others hoped to revive old glories, and when at the end of the season the Athletic Association ironically invited me to speak at their annual football banquet on "The Necessity of Gaining Circulation," I accepted, perhaps to their surprise. Accordingly, in the presence of President Hutchins and other dignitaries together with the Austin High School football team that had just won the city championship, I defended the circulation of ideas, compared the *Maroon*'s gadfly role on campus to that of Socrates in Athens, and proposed a solution to the problem of reconciling athletic with intellectual excellence by suggesting that the university buy race horses and award them a B.A. after four years of muscular effort, determining eligibility on the basis of rump measurements—those over average breadth qualifying as authentic B[ig] A[rse]s. The audience was not amused, but Hutchins later cribbed my suggestion on at least two public occasions and abolished intercollegiate football soon after I graduated.

"A chastened President" boiled down to two editorials whose punch line tells it all: "The institution he heads is not his to sacrifice for his personal ideas."[3] But as I confessed in a final editorial, "Unfortunately he [President Hutchins] was so diplomatic in his handling of the buzzing nuisance which was *The Maroon*" and of the faculty, that part of the *Maroon*'s 1937–38 editorial program was "left like a magic carpet suspended in mid air, a memento to our brash temerity."[4]

From the very start Hutchins indulged my cheekiness, and later in the year, he participated in a debate on the ends of general education organized by the *Maroon*. His opponent was a mild-mannered dean of education from Northwestern University named Ernest Melby. Mandel Hall filled to the rafters for the occasion, and loudspeakers in the Reynolds Club accommodated the overflow. I introduced the protagonists, and only once since have I spoken before so large a crowd. My mother, who sat somewhere in the rear, told me afterward that my voice carried well and was firm and mellifluous, at least to her ears. But the debate itself was a travesty. Hutchins, a skilled debater from his undergraduate years, laid verbal traps for Melby, who stumbled into them and could not begin to hold his own, any more than Plato's Thrasymachus did when debating Socrates. Yet in both cases I felt that verbal tricks supplanted serious discourse.

For the rest, the stream of editorials I spewed forth constitute a strange mix of callow exhortation and vaulting generalization—both philosophical and political—together with literary conceits and tut-tutting about disputes among other student organizations but discreet omission of all mention of clashes within the *Maroon* staff. At the time my leading role in debates then raging among Chicago undergraduates was completely engrossing, and gave me a taste for public affairs that was slow to subside. I planned first to get a Ph.D., then to write a book about a cyclical pattern of history that I was still struggling to define, after which I expected to return to public affairs in some suitably dignified role—perhaps succeeding Hutchins as president of the University of Chicago. I was ambitious, very ambitious, and my undergraduate career convinced me that anything I might wish for was probably attainable.

As for the cyclical pattern of human history lurking in the back of my mind, it gained in range and complexity as time passed, partly on the basis of my summertime reading of such authors as Freud, Tolstoy, Marx, Turgenev, and lesser lights like Lewis Mumford. History classes in my junior and senior years also exposed me to more and more information; but my teachers were uninterested in large-scale patterns, and I scorned them for their blindness. Of the numerous historians whose books I sampled, the most influential, as far as I remember, were Michael Rostovtzeff and Carl Becker. Rostovtzeff's *Social and Economic History of the Roman Empire* encouraged my effort to cycle through history since Rostovtzeff sought to explain the fall of the Roman Empire in light of the Bolshevik Revolution, which had driven him from his native land. From Carl Becker's *Heavenly City of the Eighteenth-Century Philosphers* I learned that even the most revolutionary ideas remain closely connected with what the revolutionaries were trying to reject. "Plus ça change, plus c'est la même chose," in short, had greater depth and power than contemporaries could recognize, or than I then perceived in rejecting my father's style of text-bound historical scholarship.

But the single most important stimulus to my thought came by chance when I took a summer course from Robert Redfield entitled "Folk Society." Redfield was an anthropologist, dean of the Social Sciences Division, and a man who aspired to discover general patterns of human society quite as strenuously as I did. He was then seeking to generalize from fieldwork he had done as a graduate student in Mexico, and eventually he published his ideas in a book entitled *The Folk Culture of Yucatan* (1941). But in 1936 he was still trying them out on us, which imparted unusual force and flavor to his lectures.

His approach was to set up antithetical ideal types, expecting to locate any actual human community somewhere along the spectrum of opposites his fieldwork had suggested to him. At one pole stood "folk society," approximated in a remote inland village named Chan Kom, where he had collected data for his Ph.D. thesis. There custom prevailed, most behavior was routine, even sacred, and change was almost absent, since face-to-face encounters linked everyone closely together and strangers almost never came. At the other pole stood the coastal, metropolitan city of Merida, where strangers abounded and new forms of behavior strained or violated custom, as impersonal encounters and market exchanges multiplied. Above all, Merida was a place where rival and fragmented belief systems clashed so that individuals no longer commanded effective customary responses to encounters with all the persons and things around them—a circumstance that sustained and comforted the poverty-stricken inhabitants of Chan Kom. Later, when Redfield revisited Chan Kom he realized that social change operated there too, and he wrote a book called *A Village That Chose Progress* (1950) to acknowledge the fact. But in 1936 his typology had no time dimension. Nonetheless, I was so strongly attracted to his scheme that it is scarcely an exaggeration to describe my subsequent intellectual effort as an attempt to explore the missing time dimension of social change as Redfield envisaged it, not in Yucatan but around the whole earth and across recorded time.

Redfield also introduced me to American cultural anthropology as represented by such writers as Ruth Benedict, Margaret Mead, A. R. Radcliffe-Brown, Clark Wissler, and Ralph Linton. (Oddly, for no reason I know, Alfred Kroeber was left out and I never got round to reading any of his books.) But the anthropologists whom I did read convinced me that the cake of custom was an essential support for human society and was in imminent danger of collapse in urban

America and in Europe, where Nazi expansion was already underway and another world war was clearly approaching. An irresistible cycle seemed to operate, repeating patterns of the ancient world where civil strife and war brought disaster first to Greek cities and then to the Roman republic. I surmised that patterned and predictable changes in social psychology propelled the course of events, and that those changes were in turn rooted in the very nature of civilization—the ineluctable breaker of custom and eroder of moral codes, and itself the product and expression of rapid technological and social change.

Old Greek notions of Nemesis seemed still at work. Sometime in 1938, for example, one of my teachers, David Grene, published an excerpt from one of Thucydides' speeches in the *Nation*, substituting Britain for Athens and Germany for Sparta, and, amazingly, the result was a persuasive commentary on contemporary events. Accordingly, in the summer of 1938, having graduated from the *Maroon*, I dashed off ninety-five pages entitled "Nemesis: A Study of the Rise and Fall of Civilizations." This was, of course, a trial run for my big book.

Rereading it after decades of oblivion arouses ambivalent feelings. Some sentences still strike home, yet the writing is sloppy, and reckless generalization everywhere prevails. What information I had was wholly confined to a few segments of European history. That reflected my education, for my teachers concentrated attention on ancient Athens and Sparta, then on Rome, western Europe, and its American offshoot. I later realized how their distribution of attention reflected the liberal nineteenth-century idea that personal freedom and self-government, perfected in the nineteenth century with representative legislatures and a limited magistracy, was what gave meaning to history. But my professors were uneasy with the liberal view they had inherited, and solved the awkward problem of fitting World War I into that rosy, self-flattering portrait by ending classroom history with a heated debate over the question of Germany's war guilt in 1914.

To be sure, realpolitik was another, and quite discrepant, strand in the tradition of academic history that I imbibed. That was what introduced Russia into European history at the time of Peter the Great and incorporated Turkey, India, China, and America into the vortex of European Great Power struggles at appropriate points in time. But since England and France had emerged as dominant imperial powers in the nineteenth century, contradictions between the liberal and realpolitik versions of history were, in effect, resolved by assuming, with Herodotus, that free men fight better than those subject to tyrants. As a result, power and liberty marched triumphantly together throughout recorded history—or at least ought to. Decline and fall were impossible to understand, given such assumptions. More immediately, when depression paralyzed liberal democracies, and when Nazi and Communist powers were clearly in the ascendant, such a faith was hard to sustain.

My teachers never even asked the question. Looking for meaning in history was not their business, even though what they actually taught still reflected what others had once believed. Instead they declared that scientific source criticism and exhaustion of relevant sources made written histories scientific, yes, and true forever, as long as a dutiful historian transcribed (or summarized) them accurately. On such assumptions, detail and more detail was the only direction of growth. Overall meaning, together with large-scale patterns, was either illusory or was expected to emerge spontaneously simply by juxtaposing more and more scientifically transcribed (and therefore true) monographs on library shelves. I scorned such naïveté, having gleaned from Plato that the relation between words and things was far more elusive than my history professors imagined; and from Thucydides, that history exhibited processes entirely beyond deliberate control, and which contemporaries seldom recognized.

How then could I hope to find meaningful historical truth? What I needed was a theory of social change to direct attention at what really mattered; and the anthropologists provided persuasive hints. Clark Wissler, in particular, showed me how contact with the Spanish and their array of new skills tempted or allowed Plains Indians to borrow "culture traits" from the newcomers, thereby creating tribes of horse nomads and buffalo hunters, whose cultural heritages had to be drastically remodeled to accommodate a drastically new way of life.

Borrowing from strangers and subsequent blending of old and new seemed a likely model for historic change in general. But what did that do to the cake of custom—those shared and inherited cultural meanings that intervened between individuals and the outer world, sustaining effective cooperation and a psychologically bearable daily existence for those who shared them? And what happened when different cakes of custom collided, or when they broke down? That was my overarching concern. Reversion to what? Poverty-stricken agrarian society, as I predicted in one of my *Maroon* editorials? Angry crowds rioting in city streets? Or what? Needless to say, my essay "Nemesis" did not answer that question with which, nonetheless, it concludes.

Infatuation with my own ideas and with the university environment in which they had sprouted kept me at Chicago for my M.A. But I decided to blend the two poles of my intellectual life by pursuing that degree under the Committee on the History of Culture. And since I also proposed to study ancient, medieval, and modern history for my Ph.D., I opted for a year devoted to the history, philosophy, and art of the classical Mediterranean world. Art was included because the interdepartmental committee's rules required three courses in three different departments for an M.A. That put me in the hands of an expert on Greek vase painting named Johnson, whose slides I enjoyed but whose comments on the images of Greek and Roman art were narrowly technical and, for me, trivial. I had already taken three introductory history courses from J. A. O. Larsen, Chicago's professor of ancient history, and was linguistically unqualified for his seminar, so I fell into the hands of other teachers, chief among them a new recruit to the Latin Department named Richard Bruère. His courses on Livy and Tacitus approximated the textual precision and detail (but not the intellectual stimulus) that Hutchins and Adler had lavished on Plato's *Republic*. In philosophy McKeon was king, and I have already described my eventual disillusionment with his approach.

Partly under the influence of my study of the two Roman historians, I chose to write my M.A. thesis on their Greek predecessors, entitling it "Herodotus and Thucydides: A Consideration of the Structure of Their Histories." This was a scandalously ambitious theme for a beginner to take on, but Professor Larsen reluctantly agreed to be my first reader and McKeon was my second. I wrote its hundred pages in the spring quarter while taking the normal load of three courses, thus qualifying for my M.A. degree in June 1939. This required the readers to approve my thesis in a very short time; both Larsen and McKeon had serious qualms but in the end accepted it. My inability to read Greek was one obvious problem since I sought to comprehend the two historians' organizing ideas and, for Thucydides, changes in his understanding of the wars he wrote about. I did so by inspecting the sorts of causes they adduced to explain what happened, using existing concordances of both texts to be sure of completeness and the Loeb Library editions with English and Greek texts on facing pages to pick out the exact Greek phrases used in each instance. Scholarly literature also played a large role, for others far more expert than I had discussed these texts endlessly, and I borrowed many key ideas from them. Overall, I found exactly what I expected to find, i.e., that personal assumptions shaped the overall meanings that Herodotus and Thucydides infused into their histories; and that modified, half-abandoned religious heritages lay behind their respective worldviews.

My thesis had an unusual afterlife, for when a postwar humanities course required all undergraduates to read Thucydides, someone noticed a promising title in the library catalogue and decided that what I had written was a useful shortcut for understanding their assignment. Subsequently, a modest underground developed among generations of anxious or ambitious undergraduates, keeping my thesis in active circulation for a good many years. Revisiting it more than sixty years afterward, I find my argument still plausible and recognize a far more finished level of scholarship than what earlier class papers, or the slap-dash "Nemesis" essay, had exhibited. Classical learning was, in fact, exquisitely refined by centuries of effort, and if I had not been so deficient linguistically, I might have become a classicist myself. But minute precision prevailed in classical scholarship even more than elsewhere, and I was bent, as always, on pursuing large-scale patterns. I aimed instead at finding a topic for my Ph.D. thesis in modern history, after another year of focusing mainly on the Middle Ages.

A second landmark of my M.A. year was the fact that I began actually to read books in French and German. Previously foreign language had figured in my education as a burdensome exercise in rote memorization, practiced solely in introductory language classes. I still recall exactly where I sat down in the classics library at Chicago one day and started to read an elegantly printed publication of the Royal Belgian Academy entitled *Comment la Belgique fût Romanisée* by a scholar named Cumont. I read it through at a sitting, skipping lunch as was my custom and finding that simply by reading on without pausing to look up unfamiliar words I still could follow the argument. All of a sudden I was actually reading French! Not only that: Cumont's essay told me that the smiling fields of medieval Flanders had been dark, dank forests throughout Roman times, making the Romanization he celebrated a very superficial phenomenon indeed. I suddenly realized that something important must have changed by the eleventh century when crowded villages and towns began to sprout so luxuriantly where only forests had previously existed. To discover what that might have been was therefore a prime question for me when I turned my primary attention to medieval history in 1939–40.

By now I was at last ready to imitate my younger sisters and leave home. Accordingly I shed the nurturing embrace of my mother and of my alma mater in the autumn of 1939 to become teaching assistant to Carl Stephenson, professor of medieval history at Cornell University in Ithaca, New York. Nonetheless, Carl Becker was the man who attracted me to Cornell, in accordance with advice from Louis Gottschalk, professor of modern history at Chicago, who was himself one of Becker's first Ph.D. students. I, as it turned out, was his last graduate assistant (1940–41), since Becker retired in 1941 and died in 1945 before I came back from the war.

The regimen at Cornell was very different from what I had known at Chicago. The History Department offered no graduate courses per se. Instead, graduate students were free to listen to any undergraduate lectures they wished, but were not supposed to write assigned papers or exams. Each professor also conducted a graduate seminar that met once a week. But what happened in such seminars depended entirely on each professor's good pleasure. When I showed up in the fall of 1939 Stephenson had just completed an essay on the origins of feudalism that was eventually published in the *American Historical Review*. He used his seminar to make us read some of the principal books he had used in preparing that essay—perhaps as a check on his own work. Each student was assigned a particular author. Mine was a stout volume written by a German professor named Heinrich Brunner, entitled, if I remember correctly, *Deutsche Verfassungsgeschichte*. Brunner was intent to show that feudalism was a deplorable foreign import into Germany, deriving mainly from Roman law and social practice, thereby undermining the Imperial German Reich and assuring centuries of German humiliation by the French. His sources were legal and constitutional texts; his method dry as dust and, to me, difficult to decipher from the German *schrift* in which it was presented and unconvincing to boot. I duly summarized what I understood of his argument when it was my turn to speak at the seminar, and that was that. But at Stephenson's suggestion I later looked at Marc Bloch's *Les caractères originaux de l'histoire rurale française* and found in him a scholar whose pages smelt of barnyard realities rather than of Brunner's legalisms. More than that, Bloch gave me a hint of what had transformed the flat, waterlogged plains of Belgium from Roman swamps and forests into the fertile grain fields of medieval times. I accordingly spent the rest of my first year at Cornell partly in pursuing the answer to the question Cumont had posed for me the year before and partly in tying up philosophical loose ends from my Chicago years.

Four substantial papers resulted from my labors. I entitled them

"The Springs of Plato's Thought," "Thoughts on the History of Classical Philosophy," "On Truth" (left incomplete), and "The Year 1000 A.D., Being an Inquiry into the Rise of Towns in North Western Europe." I never showed any of these to my teachers, but did submit two of them for an essay prize, whose faculty readers remained anonymous and were not impressed by either of my submissions. Nevertheless, these four papers mark a new level of scholarly attainment. Two of them still seem persuasive, almost worth publishing. The uncompleted essay "On Truth," however, was a defeat, dissolving in confusion as I struggled with the age-old question of how words relate to things.

The essay on Plato argues that what drove Plato to philosophy was the failure of his political ambitions. Descended from the royal family of Athens, he felt his proper role was to rule. But in democratic Athens political success required flattering the voters, and that Plato was not willing to do. Accordingly, frustration led to thought, as John Dewey had led me to expect, and Plato eventually took on the whole range of philosophical questions others had raised, without, however, finding clear and convincing answers that satisfied him. In particular, I convinced myself that in later life, as evidenced by such dialogues as *Gorgias* and *The Laws*, Plato did not accept the core of historic Platonism, i.e., the transcendent World of Ideas explored in *The Republic*. I was, I now realize, brashly assimilating Plato to my own philosophical posture, concerned with the pursuit of truth and unable to satisfy myself with my own or others' verbal formulations. Plato and Hutchins had become for me twin exemplars of the intellectual life—seeking truth strenuously, yet never finding words accurate enough to satisfy them for long. I will never know whether either of them actually conformed to my surmise— though for Plato this essay offers what still seems to me a quite convincing portrait of him as a man who never succeeded in finding the eternal truth he sought.

The two other philosophical essays sought to sum up what I had learned in my student years at Chicago. "History of Classical Philosophy" is too slap-dash to deserve much attention. But what I was after is serious enough: to understand the changing social-psychological roles that philosophy played in the Greco-Roman world—starting from personal inquiry into the mysterious regularities of the natural world, and then shifting attention to mysterious irregularities of human behavior, before hardening into codes of conduct (and belief) designed for gentlemen of leisure, among whom older religious ideas had become merely quaint, poetic motifs.

Both these essays were thus fundamentally historical. The third was, or sought to be, properly philosophical by attacking the problem of truth head on. In the end, after many weeks of effort, I gave up. The surviving manuscript is unreadable, thanks to innumerable corrections and incomplete insertions. Yet my approach was unusual, and indeed historical, but on an extended evolutionary time scale. I began with how amoeba rely on immediate chemical touch and taste to relate to things around them by engulfing food and rejecting what is inedible; then I took up a more complex form of life, the hydra (first encountered in the biological sciences survey at Chicago), which uses specialized sensors and flexible tentacles to bring food into its digestive cavity. I planned to solve my problem of truth by advancing to the still more complicated way in which humans relate to the world around them by using yet another kind of intermediary—words. But diversity in the use of words confused me, primarily because I failed to realize that maintenance of social cohesion and cooperation was the primary function of human words and, throughout history, had claimed precedence over a secondary—though also important—role for words, namely, filtering out sensory irrelevancies and focusing conscious attention upon (often arbitrarily) selected aspects of our nonhuman environment.

Many years later Ernest Gellner's *Plow, Sword and Book* (1989) clarified the question for me by arguing that we use words to construct an imaginary world of meanings and use those meanings to guide everyday behavior toward persons and things alike. Cooperation with persons around us, sharing the same (or almost the same) world of meanings, thereby becomes far more efficient and effective than would otherwise be possible; while contacts with things, however important for finding food and escaping enemies, are often skewed by beliefs that have little or no basis in external reality whatever.

From this point of view, the abstract search for truths about things in general was exceptional, even though it eventually turned out to be as pregnant with surprising consequences as the invention of language itself had been. For if shared meanings made human societies uniquely flexible and formidable, human science, carefully corrected by observation, experiment, and measurement, eventually multiplied our formidability many times over, with consequences for the earth's ecosystem we have only begun to experience. But in 1939–40 none of this was clear to me. I abandoned philosophy, concentrating instead on preparing to write a history that would illumine what I believed were cyclical processes governing the rise and fall of civilizations.

The fourth essay I wrote in the spring of 1940, "The Year 1000," was a start in that direction, setting forth among other things an answer to the question about the Belgian countryside that Cumont had raised for me the year before. Simultaneously my discovery offered a new angle of vision on the rise of towns in western Europe just before and after the millennium year. The rise of towns was one of Stephenson's hobby horses, derived from his years of graduate study with Henri Pirenne, and in retrospect I do not understand why I did not show my essay to him. But I kept it to myself and was duly disappointed when it failed to win the prize contest in which I had entered it.

My discovery was the mouldboard plow and how its use altered the natural contours of the north European plain, creating artificial drainage even (or especially) on flat clay soils. Artificial drainage, in turn, made it possible to raise wheat and barley—native to semi-arid hillsides of the Middle East—on the flat, rain-soaked north European plain. Watching my grandfather walk back and forth behind his plow, turning a furrow first to one side and, when returning, to the other, had already shown me how mouldboard plows work. An initial hint of their historical establishment in Europe came from Marc Bloch's *Caractères originaux*, in which he casually observed that areas of Danish settlement in Normandy featured long acre fields—the signature of mouldboard cultivation—from the start, whereas Norwegian settlements did not. He also noted that long acre fields subsequently supplanted the original squarish Norwegian fields, but without asking why.

I also profited from an article by Lynn White Jr., "Technology and Invention in the Middle Ages,"[5] celebrating among other things the invention of wheeled plows; but the really pivotal book that explained why the change took place was a strangely overlooked work by C. S. and C. S. Orwin, *The Open Fields*.[6] The Orwins were farmers, and their book described in detail how they actually managed the open fields of Laxton Manor in England, which then still retained its medieval field system. In particular, the Orwins made clear how plow lands were deliberately raised or lowered by mouldboard cultivation, depending on how the furrows were laid out, and explained how low-lying baulks between the plow lands drained the fields artificially. And, as I subsequently discovered, a well-known medieval agricultural writer, Walter of Henley, had referred to the same thing more elliptically in the thirteenth century. This then (together with the axe) was the technology that converted the dank Roman forests of the north European plain into the open fields of medieval Europe, and this was what supported townsmen and all the other trappings of medieval civilization much more abundantly than scratch-plow farming had been able to do in the classical era.

But, characteristically, in writing up my discovery I started with neolithic times and devoted most of my first sixty pages to the rise and fall of classical Mediterranean cities and civilization, summarizing ideas about the cycle of civilization I had elaborated during my M.A. year. Much of the argument now strikes me as far too bald, though not entirely wrong-headed. But the final sixteen pages of the essay, explaining what I had learned at Cornell about how peasant plow teams converted the water-logged flatlands of northwestern Europe into productive grain fields before and after the year 1000 A.D., still seem correct and fundamentally important. This was, in short, a sort of coming of age: the first of my big ideas that still remains thoroughly convincing and repeatedly figures in my later published books and articles.

This, together with the fiasco of my essay "On Truth," confirmed my choice of history as a vehicle for understanding things in general and human affairs in particular. I became content to use words as I had been apprenticed to them, without knowing for sure whether they corresponded to external reality or, mayhap, themselves created the meanings they conveyed.

Altogether, therefore, my first year away from home in 1939–40 was a solid intellectual success. In addition, I learned to live alone, surrounded by a circle of about a dozen history graduate students whose carrels in the White Library adjoined one another. We usually ate supper together at a cafeteria run by the School of Domestic Economy, where a full meal cost thirty-five cents; and I supplemented this by having afternoon coffee and a cookie for five cents with the same group of students. But I ate nothing else and not surprisingly lost weight throughout the academic year, only to fatten up again in summer when I returned home to my mother's cooking. I lived within my means, which meant paying most of my stipend (fifty dollars per month) to rent a room in a retired professor's house and pinching every leftover penny very tightly indeed. But poverty was taken for granted among graduate students in those days; and I made lasting friends of two of them, named Scott Lytle and Carl Gustavson, while Gussie Gaskill, the librarian who presided over the White Library, became a den mother to us all and was particularly kind to me, who, I suppose, needed her more than the rest.

Three further expansions of my horizon date mainly from my second year at Cornell, when I shifted attention to modern history. These were 1) the notion that dynamic equilibrium was the proper model for the largely unconscious human social processes with which I was so enamored; 2) recognition of a puzzling discrepancy between Russian and east European history and patterns familiar further west; and 3) most intoxicating and humbling of all, my encounter with hitherto unconsidered ranges of human history as set forth by Arnold J. Toynbee in the first three volumes of his *A Study of History.* Let me say a few words about each.

In 1940–41 Carl Becker was chronically ill and about to retire. Accordingly, a historian from Stanford, Professor Harris, was invited to help out in modern European history for the year. He was, I suspect, rather shocked by the lax rules for seminar work that then prevailed at Cornell. At any rate, he undertook to instruct us in note taking and other established rituals of historical research and required those who took his seminar to practice them by writing a properly footnoted paper. His seminar focused on social theorists of the nineteenth and twentieth centuries, and I was assigned (or perhaps chose?) *The Mind and Society* by Vilfredo Pareto, then newly translated into English. I duly wrote an appropriately footnoted summary of Pareto's argument and read it to the seminar when it was my turn to perform. Most of Pareto's terminology left me cold, but his claim that human society was a dynamic equilibrium, featuring simultaneous interdependence of variables, won my full assent. I had long believed that social processes prevailed over conscious purposes. Pareto's borrowing from physics offered new precision (or at least supplied a clearer metaphor) for that belief.

The image I carried over into my own thinking was of an indefinite number of elastic bands, fixed to a frame and stretched so that the resulting tension spread automatically throughout the system (read society) whenever any one band was pulled tighter or relaxed. Any such change generated wave patterns of overcorrection, and subsequent reversal, until friction compelled the disturbed system to settle down once again toward a more nearly stable equilibrium. But when disturbances from outside the system were frequent, indeed continual, as was clearly the case with urbanized human societies, the process of overcorrection and reaction became more and more turbulent, eventually threatening the integrity of the system itself. In other words, as I then conceived matters, too much rapid change could bring on collapse of civilization. The most immediate practical effect was to make me very skittish of simple "cause and effect" linkages, and I believe that I subsequently banished (or almost banished?) the words *cause* and *because* from my working vocabulary.

The second enlargement of my historical consciousness in 1940–41 was the result of hearing Philip Mosely and Marc Szeftel lecture on the history of Russia, the Balkans, and Poland. Since these were undergraduate courses, I merely listened in, but was sufficiently intrigued by what the professors were saying to read a good deal. The history of the Jews in eastern Europe, for example, was completely new. At Chicago, the Enlightenment sufficed to banish Judaism and other forms of religion from European history, especially because two of my professors of modern European history were themselves Jews who dearly wished to be wholly accepted into gentile society.

East European history raised a central question. Why did it differ so sharply from the triumphant advance toward freedom and self-government in western Europe that dominated the story to which I had been apprenticed? Why, for example, did serfdom decay in western Europe and expand in the east between 1300 and 1700? Why indeed? And how did differing religious traditions—Catholic, Protestant, Orthodox, Muslim, and Jewish—affect public behavior and private experience? Once the Reformation was left behind, my teachers had systematically side-stepped the subject, but I knew religion was central for my parents and knew also that unspoken Jewish-Gentile distinctions affected human relations in Chicago at large and at the University of Chicago in particular. Some very important things were obviously missing from my schooling.

Mosely and Szeftel therefore gave me much to wonder about and inquire into. But their impact was dwarfed by the abrupt enlargement of the historicable world that dawned upon me when I happened to notice three green-bound volumes of Toynbee's *A Study of History*[7] on the library shelves, and started to read them through.

I had been vaguely aware of Toynbee while still at Chicago. Dismissive remarks in my essay "Nemesis" show that I pigeonholed him as a twin to Spengler. But I had never read a word he had written, and unless memory deceives me, when I opened those unfamiliar green volumes, I had forgotten all about him.

At any rate, the next few days were the most enthralling encounter with the printed word I ever experienced. Again and again, Toynbee's pages opened broad new vistas of the historical past for me, and the parallel patterns of rise and fall in each of the separate civilizations he anatomized struck me as generally convincing. I was already committed to cycles and to the notion of "civilization" as a historical actor, liable to breakdown. But Toynbee's cycles were far more subtly worked out than anything I had ever imagined, and the breadth of his learning was breathtaking. I was dazzled to see how a single man had been able to take on the whole wide world and make historical sense of it! That was exactly what I wanted to do myself, but I had always naively excluded four-fifths (or more) of humankind and recorded history from my purview!

Delight, admiration, and acquiescence alternated with twinges of skepticism as I read Toynbee's volumes. In particular, my anthropological exposure to the diffusion of "culture traits" in North America made me believe that separate civilizations were not nearly as impervious to outside influences—especially technological improvements —as Toynbee claimed. But what Kant said of Hume, I can also say of Toynbee, for it was he who wakened me from my dogmatic slumbers by showing me how very many other peoples had histories that had to be fitted into any interpretive scheme that purported to be generally valid.

All too obviously, Europe and the West were not the whole of history. In some sense, I had always known that obvious fact but strangely, naively, surprisingly had never recognized the professional possibility and obligation it implied. But from then on, I knew that the big book I hoped to write would have to be a world history and would take far more extended preparation than I had envisioned for my Ph.D. course of study in ancient, medieval, and modern European history. My education, as I neared the Ph.D., was only starting.

I was, nonetheless, hasting toward thesis writing, having satisfied all other requirements for the degree by the end of my second year at Cornell. On the strength of my mouldboard plow discoveries, I decided to look for a comparable horizon in modern history and realized immediately—or almost immediately—that the spread of potato cultivation in Europe was almost as transformative as the spread of mouldboard cultivation had been in the Middle Ages. Everywhere east of the Elbe, potatoes yielded up to four times as many calories per acre as rye, the principal cereal that ripened reliably in that region. Potatoes had the further advantage of not necessarily displacing grain. For planting the tubers on previously fallowed fields and then hoeing sufficed to eliminate weeds—which was the purpose of fallowing—and simultaneously assured an abundant extra supply of very nutritious food. This was the bonanza that permitted—with other enabling factors—the rapid rise of modern industry on the European continent in the nineteenth century. How that happened was what my Ph.D. thesis set out to explain.

No professor at Cornell was in the least interested in such an inquiry, but Philip Mosely agreed to be my thesis supervisor readily enough. This choice meant turning my back on Becker, who had attracted me to Cornell in the first place. But it turned out that my roles as his teaching assistant and participant in his seminar in 1940–41 were both profoundly disappointing. Becker was ill and cancelled his seminar more often than he showed up, and asked absolutely nothing of us when it did meet. Instead he read to us from a manuscript he was working on but never bothered to explain what he was really up to. His stumbling exploration of Hindu speculations about time, therefore, rang strangely in my ears, and only years afterward did I discover that he was actually setting out to explore historiographical concepts more adequately than Harry Elmer Barnes had done in a recent book, and planning to do so on a worldwide basis. Becker, too, was therefore striving toward world history, but I entirely failed to realize what he was up to at the time.

What I saw instead was a man whose course on the French Revolution had not been altered for decades, and who lectured in a monotone, reciting over again what I had already learned first from his high school textbook and then from Professor Gottschalk at Chicago. I was appalled. Where was the probing mind and literary elegance I had expected? Why was his manuscript so mangled that he often lost his place when trying to read it to us? I remember thinking that the famous stylist had somehow forgotten how to write, for I was accustomed to rapid composition, accepting sentences as they came from my fingers almost without correction. Nowadays, I revise and revise again, and understand that the tangled manuscript Becker brought to his seminar was the price he paid for the limpid style of his finished product. But at the time I entirely failed to understand how hard it was, even for him, to find the right words to convey his meaning. In effect I only learned what not to do from the man whom Gottschalk revered.

In contrast, Mosely was young, vigorous, and a fine linguist. His Ph.D. thesis was a thoroughly traditional monograph about an episode in European diplomatic history; but he projected a (never realized) book on the South Slav *zadruga*. "Zadruga" refers to an extended family cultivating land collectively. His interests were at least partially agricultural, and that made it natural to ask him to supervise my projected plunge underground in pursuit of the role of the potato in European history.

I began reading on the general subject long before Mosely accepted my thesis proposal, and I knew full well that the central importance of the potato for modern history was the increase it brought to agricultural productivity across the north European plain—from the Loire to the Volga—more or less where the mouldboard plow had done the same thing centuries before. But when it came to more minute research, it seemed natural to start with Ireland, where the importance of the potato was notorious. Very soon it became evident that materials available at Cornell about the potato in Ireland were more than adequate for a Ph.D. thesis. At Mosely's request, I therefore composed a fifty-five-page summary of the five chapters of my projected thesis before heading for the New York Public Library, where I spent the summer of 1941 reading more and more about Irish potatoes.

Obeying the rules Professor Harris had taught me, I took innumerable notes on slips of paper, each carefully identified by source, subject, and date. Every evening I sorted the day's harvest of notes into a master file, arranged according to projected chapter headings. By the end of the summer I was ready to write, but by then the military draft was in operation, and my number came up in August 1941. In early September my Draft Board in Chicago ordered me to report for induction, so I stowed my thesis notes away and, after passing a physical exam, was duly sworn in as a private in the Army of the United States.

My formal education was not actually completed in 1941. Five years later I returned to Cornell and wrote up my thesis notes, but that was aftermath and letdown. By then new thoughts pulled in new directions. To explore them requires a new chapter.

CHAPTER 2

From Basic Training to
The Rise of the West
1941–1963

When I first put on an army uniform I expected to retain my academic habits and learn Russian in spare time. But lack of a light to read by in the barracks soon made initial gestures in that direction abortive. Altogether, I spent five years and two months on active duty, and by the time of my final discharge in November 1946, I had risen from private to captain. The variety of experiences that came my way was unusual and made me a better historian, not least by giving me insights into aspects of military organization and behavior.

Basic training as an antiaircraft artilleryman lasted three months. Most of it was farcical due to acute shortages of every sort of equipment. For the first six weeks, for example, a single set of fatigues was all the quartermaster could find to issue to us. Since it was still sweaty in Texas in September, the resulting stench was intense until eventually relieved by another set of clothing and the base laundry. Similarly, throughout my basic training, in the absence of lawn mowers, we prepared for inspection every Saturday morning by picking the grass around our barracks by hand. Above all, whenever training films ran short, illiterate corporals from the regular army drilled us day after day after day. Yet I did not resent that archaic ritual. Instead I wrote a poem about it. My generally positive reaction to drill was at least mildly puzzling at the time, and the experience eventually helped me to write *The Pursuit of Power*, where, among other matters, I explored the psychic effect of close-order drill on European armies.

Basic training was almost over when Japanese planes attacked Pearl Harbor. We were promptly ordered to San Francisco, and embarked for Hawaii on the day after Christmas, 1941. On arrival, our training units were disbanded, and we were distributed, randomly and as individuals, among Coast Artillery units to bring them up to full strength. I accordingly spent the next nine months in the regular army, manning gigantic and archaic disappearing-carriage guns that had been dug into Diamond Head sometime about 1910 and were supposed to guard Honolulu from naval attack. I thus became part of a strange collection of urban drifters, Appalachian illiterates, and other flotsam and jetsam of American society. However alien their behavior was to my previous life experiences—and it was very alien indeed—they nevertheless tolerated me and I them. After months of semi-idleness, I came away with modest insight into the lives of regular soldiers: men unable or unwilling to conform to the requirements of commercial urban society, but who nevertheless could and did lead meaningful and even successful lives within the protective chrysalis of military units that assured them of food, clothing, shelter, and companionship; and whose formal constraints and rigid hierarchy were much mollified in practice and relieved by conventional forms of licentiousness when on leave.

In due course, impersonal procedures of army personnel management packed me off to Officer Training School at Fort Monroe, Virginia, whence after three months of additional instruction, I emerged in November 1942 as a second lieutenant in the Coast Artillery Branch. I was assigned first to Puerto Rico, then to Curaçao, serving in batteries equipped with 155 mm artillery pieces left over from World War I. Pennsylvania miners and other regular soldiers from North America manned my first battery, but when they were sent home, Puerto Rican troops took their place. For more than a year, therefore, I commanded Spanish-speaking draftees whose recalcitrance to military regulations was systematic, inasmuch as family ties obliged them to leave army boots and other valuables behind when returning from leave.

My role was to hector them daily and make them conform more nearly to regulations: "Where's your cap?" and that sort of thing. By the time I got to Curaçao early in 1944 I had become a first lieutenant and found myself in command of four 155 mm guns and a company of 220 men, miles away from my superiors. Our battery was supposed to sink any German submarine that dared to attack the Curaçao oil refinery. Daily "dry run" practice did not make us truly proficient, but no submarine ever showed up to test us. In effect I was thrust into an imperialist role, commanding troops of a different culture performing quasi-peacetime garrison duty on foreign soil. Yet when in 1944 I was ordered to go to Washington, D.C., for a new, unspecified assignment, some of the men who had formed into ranks to hear the news responded by bursting into tears! I was taken aback. Mainland American soldiers would most certainly not have behaved in that way. But Puerto Rican country folk, drafted from the hills of that island, were less inhibited and, to my amazement, must have come to trust and depend on me, despite the way I chivvied them! Emotional bonding between commander and soldier was never more explicit, or more surprising. In retrospect, it still remains a high point of my life: a kind of success I had neither expected nor deserved.

Being so mysteriously ordered to report to the Pentagon illustrated another aspect of military—indeed of all bureaucratic—administration: how personal connections often govern exceptional appointments and promotions. In this case, it all dated back to a chance encounter with Professor Mosely in Puerto Rico, just before my transfer to Curaçao. He had, by then, left Cornell for the State Department, and his proficiency in Russian was such that he went to the Moscow Conference, 18–30 October 1943, serving as translator and advisor to the American secretary of state, Cordell Hull. En route back to Washington Mosely spent the night at Borinquen Field in Puerto Rico, where I was then stationed. I saw him there as he walked into the officers' mess, and spent the balance of the evening conversing with him about Tito, Mihailovich, and related Balkan matters. As a result, when Ambassador Lincoln MacVeagh, then based in Cairo, Egypt, and accredited to the Greek and Yugoslav governments in exile, requested the State Department to find an assistant military attaché for his staff, the matter came to Philip Mosley's attention. Remembering our meeting, he promptly nominated me and his suggestion eventually prevailed, with the surprising results just mentioned.

Once arrived at the Pentagon, I underwent a short course in cryptography and diplomatic protocol, before flying to Cairo via the South Atlantic, going from Belem to Ascension Island, and then across Africa from Accra to Khartoum and Cairo. I was an April Fool's present for Ambassador MacVeagh, arriving on 1 April 1944, and was very hospitably received by the military attaché, Col. Sterling Larrabee, who soon began to treat me rather like a son. Ambassador MacVeagh, who read everything officially forwarded from his embassy, also found my reports acceptable, and sometimes even valuable.

Until November 1944 I remained in Cairo, then went to Greece, where the German army was at last withdrawing. There I had a jeep at my disposal and so became a roving reporter for the embassy, traveling far and wide throughout the country, camping out at night more often than not, and talking to a miscellany of provincial officials—Greek and British officers, operatives of OSS (Office of Strategic Services, the American spy teams of World War II), officials of the United Nations Relief and Rehabilitation Administration, and anyone else who came across my path. I was often but not always accompanied by a Greek driver who helped out as interpreter, for I never learned to speak Greek well enough to do more than ask directions or order a meal. But a great many people in Greece— including returned emigrants—spoke broken English or French, and good will and lively curiosity nearly always sufficed to bridge linguistic barriers. Between trips I stayed in Athens and there witnessed at close hand the abortive Communist-led revolt and ensuing civil war of December 1944–February 1945.

Until June 1946, I remained at my post, and after Colonel Larrabee went home in 1945, I was twice in interim command of the military attaché office, with a DC-3 airplane at my disposal. The crew was eager for air time to keep their flight pay coming. I therefore used the plane for rather frivolous trips to Cairo, Sofia, and Naples, picking up supplies and exchanging gossip with fellow intelligence officers. What a delightful little empire I came to enjoy! There was also the equally enjoyable job of relaying to army intelligence officers in Washington whatever struck me as worthy of their attention.

Most of what I wrote officially was about personalities and politics, within and outside the ranks of the Greek army—episodic, superficial froth, but engrossing enough at a time when Marxist revolution threatened to erupt and when violent nationalists opposed the Communists more effectively than moderates of any stripe.

What better field experience could a historian have than to find himself observing revolution and counterrevolution close-up, with privileged access to leading figures of Greek society, almost all of whom—including Communists—were eager in those days to speak with an American official? I was uniquely situated to talk freely with generals and government ministers—who came and went with kaleidoscopic rapidity—as well as with members of the educated elite of Athens and the provinces and even, on some occasions, with peasants, whose way of life was still vigorously alive and had changed little since the eighteenth century or before. The United States was then an observer in Greece, not an actor. The embassy was mildly critical of British management of Greek affairs, while at least officially endeavoring to maintain cooperation with both our Russian and British allies. Greek Communists and their fellow travelers were correspondingly ambivalent, desirous of winning American support yet expecting American capitalists to come down on the British and Greek Nationalist side. Openness—indeed warmth—toward Americans prevailed throughout Greek society, and the extravagant, sometimes embarrassing hospitality with which I was received—even in starving villages—was far greater than I deserved.

I also witnessed the emotional intensity of Greek politics very close up. For example, one morning in 1945 I drove into Kilkis, a town in northern Greece, arriving by design about half an hour ahead of the approaching Greek army. Kilkis had been under Communist control for more than a year, and the Communist-led town council received me enthusiastically, explaining how they had been duly and democratically elected and deserved to remain in office. Then came the marching men of the newly organized and only half-trained National Guard Battalions, who forcibly expelled the councillors from the town hall despite their angry protests, while a sullen, suspicious crowd of citizens passively watched the change of regime. My presence may have diminished—or postponed—beatings and other violence that often accompanied such transfers of power, but the little provincial drama was poignant and powerful enough, since the fear, hatred, and anxious uncertainty prevailing on both sides was patent before my eyes.

Looking back, I find it amazing how lucky I was throughout my army years. Each experience lasted just long enough to become familiar and invite comparison with other, historical times and places, without ever exposing me to personal suffering or danger. The real face of war came close during the fighting in Athens between British and Greek guerrilla forces in 1944–45; but Americans were not officially engaged, and though I heard innumerable bullets fly past and witnessed sudden death close-up on two occasions, I was never wounded myself and actually crossed the firing lines on several occasions in order to visit an American air force unit that was isolated in a hotel in Athens, just outside the British perimeter within which the American Embassy and most government offices were located. How lucky can one be? I surely stretched the envelope without deliberately trying, simply by doing what was expected of me in the diverse situations I confronted.

Early in 1946, as return to civilian life approached, it occurred to me that I might write a book about events in Greece during World War II. Accordingly, I interviewed key figures from across the political spectrum, gathering personal impressions of some of the principal actors by quizzing them about various historical details. I also collected a few reports written by British as well as by American observers and participants. But, like Herodotus before me, I relied mainly on oral communication and personal memories of things seen. The result was my first published book, *The Greek Dilemma; War and Aftermath* (1947).[1] I composed it in exactly thirteen busy days immediately after my return to the United States on 4 July 1946 and subsequently revised part of it by condensing two introductory chapters into one to please the editor who had accepted it.

In spite of my haste and entire ignorance of important secret deals that Churchill made with Stalin over Greece and the Balkans in October 1944, this book still holds up pretty well. The narrative of what happened on the Greek political-military scene is generally accurate, and my judgments about motives, hopes, and fears are quite plausible. The book was, I believe, the first in any language to deal with contemporary Greek affairs, which were swiftly becoming one of the foci of the Cold War, and was correspondingly well received in both America and England and even in Greece. But I soon realized that reviewers from Left and Right habitually confirmed their personal predilections by selecting what pleased them from my prose. A reasonable facsimile of what I thought I had said rarely showed up in their remarks. Historical writing, I concluded, is a very inexact way of transmitting information, much less truth. Reviews of my subsequent books, even the most laudatory, have done nothing to alter my initial, rather dismaying, encounter with the pervasive inexactitude of supposedly professional communication.

The reason I wrote *The Greek Dilemma* so hastily was personal. In Athens I met Elizabeth St. John Dukinfield Darbishire (to list her full moniker), and when I discovered that her father was so close a friend to Toynbee that he was known to her as "Uncle Toynbee," I took notice. After a few months of courtship I asked her to marry me and she consented. She had grown up partly in Kentucky, where her father had inherited a farm, and partly in Greece, where he taught English at Athens College for several years before the war. She then earned a B.A. in linguistics at Swarthmore College in 1943 before getting a job as secretary in the Office of War Information (OWI). That organization brought her to Greece in 1944, where her ability to speak colloquial modern Greek and her general capability turned her into a librarian, responsible for the public face of OWI, namely, for all the books and magazines made available to the Greek public. And by the time she gave up her post and came home to marry me she had been transmuted into a Foreign Service officer in a rechristened agency, the United States Information Service.

Elizabeth's linguistic capabilities far exceeded mine. She spoke Greek, French, and German fluently, as well as broken Italian and Spanish and a smattering of Turkish. Such capabilities brought a new awareness of words into my life. Looking up derivations and cognates became a habit at the dinner table, and she became my most reliable proofreader, critic, and collaborator, especially when writing about Greece. In due course she nurtured our four children with wisdom and success. When they no longer needed her full-time attention, she took charge of a neighborhood secondhand clothing shop, run on behalf of the Laboratory Schools, and became a regular volunteer at the University of Chicago Children's Hospital. All the while she kept house, entertained guests, drove her less accomplished neighbors to and from the grocery store, and allowed me to teach and write, and did so cheerfully, competently, consistently. Her support meant that I could wend my way among the historical questions that interested me with quiet mind, freed from everyday anxieties. After the first years, her collaboration in editing my writings diminished, but she always remained at least quizzically tolerant, even of my most far-fetched investigations.

Returning to Cornell in the autumn of 1946 with a new wife and my first book in process of publication was a curious kind of decompression, transformed, as I was, from about-to-be published author and privileged official representative of the American government to mere graduate student. I was something of a loose cannon, since my most important prewar professors were all gone, and my thesis had long been forgotten. But Becker's successor, Edward Fox, took me on all the same, and the GI Bill excused the department from finding the fifty dollars per month of fellowship money that had sustained me before the war. I listened in on Fox's seminar and took a course in Russian language, but spent most of my time writing my Ph.D. dissertation. To give credit where credit is due, the note taking Professor Harris had so meticulously insisted on proved its worth, for I found it quite easy to spread out a thicket of notes for the next chapter, sort them into smaller piles, and then write away, using one note after another as the basis for a sentence or paragraph. Indeed it became something of a game to figure out where I could squeeze in reference to an unused note, and in the end, if I remember right, only about two dozen slips of paper went back into the master file, uncited and unsung.

Nevertheless, both when taking notes before the war and when writing them up in 1946–47, I found details of Irish economic, social, and agricultural history disappointingly dull, and my sources endlessly repetitious. Nineteenth-century bureaucratic reports on the Irish question were tedious to wade through, and trying to figure out potato varieties from the confusion of popular usage was less than engrossing. Partly for that reason, I was in no haste to turn my thesis into a book, which would have required a year or more in Irish and English libraries. A second subsidiary reason for dropping my thesis was of course that what I had written about was not what I had intended to inquire into when I began my research. But the thought of writing a proper history of the potato by replicating the dullness of Irish sources with the dullness (and linguistic obstacles) of parallel French, Dutch, and German—not to mention Polish and Russian—sources simply appalled me. That was not what I wanted to devote my life to, and when I eventually returned to the topic in 1998 by writing an article, setting forth my ideas about the importance of the potato in European and world history, I did so, like Bayard, without fear and without research, in response to an invitation to participate in a conference on food at the New School for Social Research in New York.[2] A flurry of other brief articles on the subject followed, but that is as far as I ever went in realizing my original Ph.D. project.

All the same, my detour into Irish history was not entirely wasted. I was reminded of the steep and enduring gradient within the British Isles between London and the barbarous Celtic fringe, whence my ancestors had emerged in the 1770s. And I did correct some facts, most notably the oral tradition that credited Walter Raleigh with introducing potatoes into Ireland, and proved beyond all reasonable doubt that anonymous Spanish (actually Basque) sailors had done so. My evidence for this assertion saw print in the *Journal of Modern History*.[3] This, my first learned journal publication, has, I believe, remained wholly unnoticed by historians of Ireland.

Soon after *The Greek Dilemma* came out, and before I had finished writing my thesis, the Twentieth Century Fund invited me and my wife to join a well-known journalist named Frank Smothers in writing a book to explain to the American public what was happening in Greece. Guerrilla war had again broken out in that country, and negotiations leading to the Truman Doctrine were in full swing. The United States was about to take over from Britain in Greece; and a trustee of the Twentieth Century Fund, then serving as assistant secretary of state, persuaded his colleagues to undertake a study to explain why the United States was plunging into such a risky foreign adventure.

Smothers had been a foreign correspondent in China before the war and was a warm admirer of Mao's land reforms in Yenan. For him, Greek guerrillas were more of the same; and his sympathy for them was a far cry from what I inherited from my months in the American Embassy. Consequently, our collaboration was strained from the start. As senior author he was in charge, and to give him his due, Smothers was eager to see for himself and was ready to take risks that a man of mature years ought not to have done. As for my wife and myself, we were young and foolish; so under his direction we traversed the roads of Greece in a rented jeep, despite the mines that infested them, and crossed into guerrilla territory on two separate occasions. Once we slept on a mountaintop as guests of a guerrilla band near Volos, only to be arrested by a very angry Greek army officer when we came down next morning. Later we spent most of a day in a village near the Albanian border while two guerrilla boy-soldiers waited uncertainly for a messenger to return from headquarters with instructions as to whether we were honored guests or prospective prisoners. But the messenger failed to return before we were ready to drive away, so the two rifle-toting guerrillas—no more than twelve to fourteen years of age—hastily concurred with the local villagers, who had decided from the start that we were honored guests.

These encounters with Greek guerrilla bands, and with the villagers who actually (and sometimes reluctantly) gave them the food they needed daily, led me to understand for the first time how and why guerrilla fighting had become a Balkan tradition. When we talked with local inhabitants of the mountains of northern Greece, they habitually described their situation in terms of the number of months local food supplies sufficed to feed their village and the number of months when outside food had to be imported. There were three, and only three, ways of doing so: 1) by buying food with cash remittances from relatives living abroad, 2) by working as harvesters and at other kinds of migrant labor in return for payments in money or in kind, or 3) by taking arms and seizing food from plains dwellers by force and threat. Such brigandage was, in turn, justified by invoking any convenient political ideology—whether national liberation from the Turks in the eighteenth and nineteenth centuries, or social justice and Communist revolution in the twentieth.

I owed this insight to the encounters with real-life Greek guerrillas that Frank Smothers sought out for us. It is a real debt, but at the time, it was disfigured by persistent disagreements about how to report what we heard and saw. He took political slogans at face value and came to believe that peasants of the plains supported the guerrillas willingly because they shared the same political convictions. My doubts found expression in a single footnote. Moreover, it soon developed that Smothers was incapable of organizing his materials into a coherent book, and in the end the Twentieth Century Fund hired a rewrite man to edit what became a scatter box of impressions and information, entitled *Report on the Greeks*.[4] Even so, the published book harbored a distressing number of footnotes and counter-footnotes in which Smothers and I aired our differences. I resolved never again to write a book in collaboration with another person.

By the time this misbegotten volume came out, I had completed my Ph.D. and, after writing a letter to President Hutchins asking for a job, was appointed instructor in the College of the University of Chicago, starting in the fall of 1947. I remained a faculty member at Chicago for the next forty years. There all but one of my children were born, and there I wrote most of my books. I found it a supportive environment and never wished to be elsewhere, even though academic storms sometimes blew very strong on our campus and I took part in most of them.

The college had been reorganized during and immediately after the war, better to embody President Hutchins's ideal of liberal education, though Richard McKeon was in practice the presiding intellect behind most of the new courses. The curriculum was in a sense inhospitable for a historian, since, with Aristotle, McKeon believed that history was the least philosophical of the sciences, being merely a chronological assemblage of information that other disciplines could perhaps use theoretically. Accordingly, history figured in the curriculum as a form of literature, studied in the Humanities II course by reading excerpts from a handful of famous historians— Gibbon and Trotsky chief among them. But when it turned out that Chicago graduates had no idea whether Luther came before or after the Declaration of Independence, or whether Cicero and Plato were contemporaries, the graduate departments in the humanities and social sciences protested. To correct this defect, I was hired to help organize a new course known as History of Western Civilization, which, after intensive and sometimes angry debate, eventually supplanted an older, established course in the required curriculum.

I accordingly started out teaching Humanities II and serving as a member of the faculty committee charged with designing and teaching an experimental version of the new history course. We were a motley crew, comprising a handful of German refugees and others whose backgrounds were quite different from mine and from one another's. Perhaps for that reason, the course we generated proved to be the most long-lived and successful of the courses the Hutchins college ever offered. Western Civ still survives at Chicago and, as far as I know, still uses the handbook I wrote in 1949 to link together all the separate readings that constituted the backbone of the course.

For the next seven years, teaching History of Western Civilization meant that year after year I explored anew high points of the European past, from ancient Greece to the twentieth century, and attended staff meetings every week where we debated how best to treat the next week's assigned readings in class. In spare time we searched for new and better readings, translated texts from ancient and modern languages to be used in next year's revised course, and in general rubbed off on one another. German modes of thought became more familiar to me through these encounters. I particularly remember teaching Ernst Troeltsch's essay "Renaissance and Reformation" and how that plunge into *Geistesgeschichte* both attracted and puzzled me. How did he know so much? Did abstract nouns like *Renaissance* really act like persons? Meanwhile, the fact that McKeon and a majority of the college faculty remained suspicious of historians' claims to intellectual respectability kept us on our toes, as a more friendly intellectual climate would not have done. So it was a splendid environment in which to widen and deepen the historical learning to which I had already been apprenticed.

I dashed off *The Handbook of Western Civilization* (1949)[5] while teaching full time—one of only two books written under the sort of distraction from which my father suffered when writing almost all of his. My method was to keep a standard textbook open on the desk beside me to check dates and the like, while balancing a portable typewriter on my knees and summarizing from my head what I had learned from my Ph.D. studies. Every so often I also insinuated an idea of my own. The *Handbook* has since been repeatedly revised, most recently in 1986. In spite of what must be increasing obsolescence, at the time I am writing it still sells several hundred copies a year, making it the longest-lived of any book I ever wrote.

But teaching Western Civ was not the way to prepare for writing the world history I planned, and when in the seventh year, sitting in a staff meeting, I knew before he started speaking what one of my most respected colleagues was going to say, I realized that diminishing returns had set in. Therefore I welcomed an invitation from the History Department to join its ranks and start teaching graduate students on a regular basis. (I had put my nose into the History Department from the start, being advised by Professor Gottschalk to insist that I should have the right to teach a course in Balkan history during one quarter of each year.) Nonetheless, after joining the department full time I kept a foothold in the college and continued to teach undergraduates, whose willingness to be surprised and readiness to challenge what I said were always tonic to me.

My early years at Chicago were interrupted in 1951–52 when, in response to an invitation from Arnold Toynbee, I went to London to write a book for the Royal Institute of International Affairs. Between 1923 and 1938 Toynbee had personally written an annual *Survey of International Affairs*. The series was suspended during the war, and Toynbee decided not to resume the task in peacetime, wishing to devote his main effort to finishing his massive *A Study of History*. But he did persuade the Rockefeller Foundation to fund what was colloquially referred to as the "War Time Survey," and I was one of a multiplicity of authors he recruited for that purpose.

This invitation is another illustration of how profoundly personal connections affected my career. I first met Toynbee in March 1947 through the courtesy of my father-in-law, Robert Shelby Darbishire, at his house in Kentucky. This was the moment when Toynbee's reputation in the United States suddenly soared into the stratosphere on the strength of Henry Luce's enthusiasm for his rebuttal to Marx, as trumpeted to the world by *Time* magazine in a cover story on 17 March 1947—exactly five days after the Truman Doctrine had been proclaimed in Washington. Robert Darbishire and Toynbee had been close friends as undergraduates at Balliol College, Oxford, and when I heard that the man who had so powerfully affected my historical ambitions would visit my father-in-law, I contrived to join the party.

That first encounter was a delight. Toynbee amazed me by the casual way he was then composing an essay Luce had commissioned —an essay paid for but never printed since it failed to endorse Luce's own grandiose vision of the coming "American century." Toynbee seemed quite unaware of the power the Luce publications then exerted in American society, and I was flattered by his courtesy in discussing current affairs and historical questions with me. He also impressed me by the way he looked at the Kentucky countryside— seeking traces of Indian and frontier life, for example, when visiting buffalo licks and Appalachian farms he remembered from earlier visits. I had never before met anyone who looked at the American landscape as a palimpsest of the human past. He did so automatically, as it were, since he was accustomed to doing the same in England, Greece, and wherever else he traveled.

I may have impressed him favorably, or maybe his invitation to me was only the result of Toynbee's reliance on personal connections to recruit writers for the "War Time Survey," some of whom were ill-equipped for the task. When I duly showed up in August

1950, I well remember the hesitancy with which Toynbee invited me to take on the core topic of Allied Great Power relations, 1941–46. He asked for a sample chapter, fearing perhaps that I would stumble. Then after I had duly submitted it for his inspection, he invited me to continue—perhaps with a sense of relief.

For the next two years I worked directly under his supervision and saw him almost every day in the basement canteen where the staff met twice a day to warm up by drinking coffee at 11 A.M. and again at 3 P.M. Fueling our bodies against the cold was very necessary, since weak electric heaters were no match for the open window insisted on by the lady with whom I shared an office high under the eaves. My fingers often stiffened from the cold after sitting at my desk for a few hours; but that did not prevent me from making steady progress on what turned out to be a 768-page volume, *America, Britain and Russia: Their Cooperation and Conflict, 1941–1946* (1953).[6]

Like *The Greek Dilemma*, this book is a quite conventional political history; and like its predecessor it stands up well in retrospect, even though some important aspects of war-time diplomacy—for example, the decipherment of secret codes—remained entirely unknown to me. At the time, however, the book attracted little attention, being buried within a series of miscellanies, some rather shoddy, that constituted the "War Time Survey" as it emerged volume after volume from Toynbee's makeshift production line. It did however win me tenure at Chicago, where I was promoted to the rank of associate professor of history in 1955.

The principal basis for *America, Britain and Russia* was a collection of newspaper clippings meticulously maintained by the library staff of the Royal Institute of International Affairs. Each day a corps of young women clipped a dozen or more leading newspapers from western Europe and the United States and sorted the clippings into boxes, arranged according to ever-shifting, well-chosen categories. As a result, I could ask for what they had about, say, the Yalta Conference, or any other diplomatic episode, and immediately receive scores of pre-sorted contemporary accounts. Under such circumstances, note taking was unnecessary. Instead I wrote my book with relevant newspaper clippings spread out on my desk, supplemented by purchased copies of the handful of published memoirs then available. This experience emboldened me to dispense with note taking in 1954 when I actually got round to trying to write the world history I had projected ever since reading Toynbee's first volumes. That turned out to be the main thing I learned from the time I spent under his supervision.

His own method was different, featuring lengthy notes—often verbatim transcriptions of a paragraph or longer—collected into bound notebooks and arranged not by subject matter but seriatim and according to the sequence of his reading. That did not seem very promising to me in 1954 because I had no idea when I started in on prehistory—a subject almost totally unknown to me—what to pay attention to and what to disregard. But I did have the advantage of a library system at Chicago that allowed faculty members to keep books on their desks indefinitely or until someone else put in a request for them. I soon discovered that I could remember for about six weeks where I had seen something that interested me. By skimming as many books and articles as possible within that span of time, ever on the alert for whatever struck me as of key importance, I was able to get an idea of what mattered most and choose what to write about, footnoting my pages with easy accuracy by having the relevant sources open before me as I composed the footnote.

More than six weeks of initial reconnaissance turned out to be a waste of time, because forgetting began to outbalance worthwhile incoming information. So even if no definite pattern of understanding had emerged spontaneously, I made it a habit to stop reading after six weeks, collect my thoughts, and make a concerted effort to outline the prospective chapter I was working on. Sometimes it took several days for an appropriate architectonic to emerge. But by persisting for two or three days, what had been an impenetrable confusion one day, embodied in fragmentary outlines and lists of things to be taken into account, suddenly took intelligible form. This commonly occurred in a flash when sitting down in the morning after a good night's sleep, thanks, presumably, to unconscious nighttime mental activity. To be sure, such moments of illumination often demanded further reading about aspects of the chapter ahead; and that in turn required minor modification of the initial outline. But that was comparatively easy to accomplish once the basic structure of each successive chapter had emerged.

This intellectual effort to make sense of the human past, chapter by chapter, was the most strenuous and sustained task I ever undertook. It required eight years during which time I only published a small, journalistic book about contemporary Greece. But I had support within the university. When, for example, I told him about my project, President George Beadle said something to the effect that he was glad I was working on the sort of history he could understand. Within the department I benefited from backing by the senior European historian at Chicago, Professor Louis Gottschalk. His own personal magnum opus, a biography of Lafayette, had just suffered irremediable disaster because an elderly French noblewoman refused to let him see some of Lafayette's papers that were still sequestered in her attic. Gottschalk had set out to exhaust all the relevant sources, so this rebuff ruined his hope of achieving a definitive, exhaustive, and eternally true account of Lafayette's life. His whole enterprise died on the spot, and he reacted by agreeing to edit a volume of the UNESCO-sponsored *Scientific and Cultural History*, which purported to be worldwide in scope. I feel pretty sure that I would have undertaken my big book with or without Gottschalk's approval, but his sympathy for my overweening ambition certainly made the initial plunge easier to take.

I also had the inestimable advantage of time off from teaching, which postwar foundations made possible for American academics as never before. Accordingly, I started my big book in 1954–55 on the strength of a grant from the Ford Foundation for "faculty enhancement." But a whole year of isolation from contacts with colleagues and students was more than I found comfortable, and in actual fact I subsequently had to scrap much of what I wrote in that first year. Once again, serendipity intervened—this time in the form of an invitation to take part in a joint Chicago-Frankfurt seminar, designed to bring German and American academics together after the Nazi disruption. From March to May 1956, I found myself at the University of Frankfurt, responsible for preparing an essay for a conference entitled "Klassicizmus und Kulturverfall," to be read before a joint German-American professorial seminar.[7] This required me to brush up my German as never before, and I depended on the Austrian-born wife of a colleague from Chicago to translate my essay into proper German and drill me on pronunciation before its presentation. Those months at Frankfurt also gave me occasion to explore German and Austrian scholarship on Eurasian history, and I soon discovered that nomads of the steppes were far more important than I had previously understood.

When I got back to Chicago and wished to start again on my big book, I recognized that most of what I had written needed fundamental revision in light of the prewar German scholarship that I had explored under the guidance of Fraulein von Dechend, *assistent* to Willi Hartner, professor of the history of science at Frankfurt and herself a formidable scholar. It was obvious that I would need more than summertime writing if I were ever to finish. I accordingly applied to the Carnegie Foundation, proposing a five-year grant that would give me six months each year to read and write. That was as long as I thought I could work continuously and with maximum efficiency on my book. Fortunately, the foundation said yes, so from 1957–62 I alternated between six months of ordinary academic duties and six months of intensive work on the big book.

This is the place to record an extraordinary quadrille I engaged in with Leften Stavrianos, a professor of history at Northwestern University. Our two schools were traditional rivals within the Chicago metropolitan community. Oddly enough, Stavrianos had been born a few years before me in Vancouver, and during the war he worked as an intelligence analyst for the Office of Strategic Services in Washington, where he read my reports from Greece. Then in 1948 I was asked to referee an article about the Greek civil war that he had submitted to the *Slavic and East European Review.* I disagreed with many of his judgments, and the editor then asked me to write a parallel piece presenting my own point of view. Our articles therefore appeared together in 1949, flatly contradicting each other. Then, when I had begun to teach Balkan history at Chicago I considered undertaking a general history of the Balkans, since the only book then available in English on the subject had been written shortly after World War I and was mainly a diplomatic history. But long before I was ready to write, Stavrianos came out with *The Balkans since 1453,*[8] and I decided he had done the job for me.

Subsequently we met face-to-face when the history faculties

of Chicago and Northwestern inaugurated annual joint dinners. Stavrianos, as befitted a man of Greek extraction, was an exuberant and generous host. But we remained wary of one another: he was a Marxist, and I a reactionary, at least in his eyes. I had no inkling that he was contemplating writing a world history until I got a letter from the Carnegie Foundation addressed to me on the outside and to Professor Stavrianos on the inside, saying that his grant for writing what became his very successful world history textbook had been approved. I forwarded it to him and soon after received the parallel letter to me which had been addressed to him. The person who put the wrong envelopes around our letters must have wondered at the convergence of our enterprises; what the officers of the Carnegie Foundation made of it I never asked. These career intersections do seem as surprising as the absence of any effort at real communication between us about either Balkan or world history. But then, we were rivals and knew it from the beginning.

Now, to return to the story of my magnum opus. After reworking most of the first year's manuscript in the light of my Frankfurt experience, I found that I could count on writing a new chapter every three months, although when my fourth child was born in May 1957, I fell a little short of that pace. Nonetheless, early in 1962 I completed the thirteenth and final chapter. But the resulting text was too long to be printed as a single volume. I took this seriously since the value of the book lay in its perspective on things in general, and multivolume works are ordinarily consulted but not read. I therefore thought it necessary to edit my manuscript down by about 20 percent to fit a one-volume format. That took most of the year, and as I cut out precious passages and tried to disguise the self-inflicted wounds that resulted, I often felt that I was damaging the readability of my book. But I persisted anyway and duly submitted a slenderized 1,100-page manuscript to the University of Chicago Press late in 1962.

I typed the manuscript of *The Rise of the West* on a portable Underwood noiseless typewriter that my parents had given me as a twenty-first birthday present. It was accompanied by a verse my father composed inviting me to use it to "write a book of lasting worth." I still possess the machine and take satisfaction in the thought that I did perhaps use it to realize my father's hope. Yet in fact most of the typing was done by a graduate student named Jean Whitenack, who, year after year, copied and recopied my mangled typescripts with altogether unusual precision and speed. Without her skillful support I could not have completed all those revisions as smoothly as we did in those pre-computer days.

Toynbee's influence, and a long tradition behind him, dictated my choice of separate civilizations as principal actors on the world historical scene. On the other hand, I abandoned the cyclical patterns that had been so dear to me in youth, emphasizing instead the continual innovative effect of contacts and exchanges between civilizations and peoples round about, with special attention to technological transfers in accordance with what I had learned from Redfield and other anthropologists. This was my principal difference from Toynbee; but efforts to explore the issue in conversation over coffee in London never got very far. In 1950–51 Toynbee was no longer interested in new ideas. Instead he was striving a bit desperately to spell out every jot and tittle of the scheme he had set out for himself almost thirty years before so as to get the last four volumes of *A Study of History* finally off his chest. To my surprise, he did so with apparent indifference not only to my queries and objections, and to everyone else's, but also to contradictions that had developed in his own views.

My association with Toynbee between 1951 and 1952 was therefore like breaking with a father figure for a second time. I found flaws in him as I had earlier found flaws in my own father. And when, after his death, Mrs. Toynbee invited me to write his biography, I found other, more serious flaws than those I had recognized in the 1950s. *Arnold J. Toynbee: A Life* (1989)[9] was therefore a difficult and disappointing book to write, for my praise of the enlargement he brought to historical consciousness—however heartfelt—was effectually eclipsed by my account of the self-betrayal and subsequent cover-up of which he was guilty during and after World War I, when he used a phony medical excuse to dodge military service and escape the horror and misery of the trenches.

Ironically enough, the reception of my own big book, which I entitled *The Rise of the West: A History of the Human Community* (1963),[10] depended directly on my break with Toynbee. For when the *New York Times* submitted it for review to Professor Hugh Trevor-Roper, he hailed it as a refutation of Toynbee's view that Western civilization had been a guilty aggressor against other civilizations. In 1957, as newly appointed Regius Professor of History at Oxford, Trevor-Roper had caricatured Toynbee's post-war prophetic and religious bent in a savage article in *Encounter*. Six years later, he used my book to belabor Toynbee afresh, praising my work extravagantly. Here are his words: "This is not only the most learned and most intelligent, it is also the most stimulating and fascinating book that has ever set out to recount and explain the whole history of mankind. . . . To read it is a great experience. It leaves echoes to reverberate, and seeds to germinate in the mind." That rhapsody appeared on the front page of the *New York Times Book Review* a few weeks before Christmas, and thanks to Trevor-Roper, my book briefly became a best seller and also won the National Book Award in History and Biography the next year.

I still cringe at his extraordinary praise. On the one hand, I agree that my book was a more nearly adequate world history than any before. On the other, I am well aware that my detailed, philological learning was far inferior to Toynbee's and to that of innumerable other redoubtable scholars. I also believe that my interpretation of how distant and different societies interacted with one another was superior to anything before. But the book also has serious defects, some of which I pointed out in a review essay published in the *Journal of World History* (1990)[11] and appended to the most recent edition of the book. My most important subsequent books were, in fact, efforts to correct a few of those defects, and can be described as extended footnotes to *The Rise of the West*. It therefore remains central to my intellectual career: a book toward which everything before contributed, and from which much (not all) of what I have subsequently thought and done descends. Overall I am very proud of the book and find myself tempted to endorse Trevor-Roper's hyperbole—though it also embarrasses me.

Among the innumerable discoveries my years of work on *The Rise of the West* entailed, three encounters stand out in retrospect. One was with Ludwig Bachofer, whose writing about Chinese bronzes convinced me that art could indeed serve as a historical source, sensitively reflecting social changes in what, I must admit, remains only a metaphorical fashion. But thenceforth I have tried to look at visual art as well as at texts when inquiring into the past. I also spent considerable effort selecting illustrations for *The Rise of the West* in hope of using them to reinforce and give greater immediacy to what I had to say in words.

Of the books I read and consulted, the most attractive for me was Fernand Braudel's *La Méditerranée* in its original 1949 edition. What made that book so powerful was the way it expanded and sharpened my previous understanding of Mediterranean landscapes and the patterns of human occupancy of plain, hill, and shore. I had touched on the subject when writing about contemporary Greece, but never saw the whole of which Greece was a part, nor imagined its historical depth and significance, until I read Braudel.

Among the colleagues I rubbed shoulders with at Chicago, the most important was Marshall G. S. Hodgson. He was a few years younger than I and had been trained as an Islamist by Gustave von Grunebaum in the Oriental Institute. When I came to know him, he was teaching a newly established course on Islamic civilization in the college and writing a handbook for that course that eventually turned into his three-volume posthumous masterpiece, *The Venture of Islam.*[12] I was aware that he had published an essay on world history in a UNESCO-sponsored journal; but he never told me, and I did not realize until after his death in 1968, that his central ambition was identical with my own—to write a real world history.

Hodgson joined the faculty as a member of the Committee on Social Thought, whose office was adjacent to my own in the Social Science building, so we saw one another casually in the hall from time to time. I recall standing outside my office one day discussing with him whether Akbar's religious policies in India were designed to navigate between clashing Safavi and Ottoman forms of Islam. I thought it probable; Hodgson scouted my idea, but having failed to convince me with his initial rebuttal, he suddenly broke off our debate, explaining that this was his lunch hour and he ought to be studying the Turkish language instead of arguing with me. In similar informal fashion we also talked about the "gunpowder empires" of the fifteenth and sixteenth centuries, and I think it possible that he invented that now familiar phrase. It certainly arose in course of our discussions and I am sure that was where I first heard—and promptly adopted—it.

If so, this is the only distinct debt I am aware of owing to Marshall Hodgson. There were barriers between us. He was a devout Quaker and a theist, while I was neither. He liked to be pedantically correct in transliterations from Arabic and other languages, while I preferred inexact familiar forms of proper names. Perhaps he was bothered to find that I was ahead of him in writing the sort of world history he aimed at. He wrote freely but clumsily, and died before finishing *The Venture of Islam*, much less his world history. Four years of devoted effort by a junior colleague, Reuben W. Smith, brought *Venture* into publishable shape; and Edmund Burke III later worked over his fragmented world historical writings and published some of them in 1993, under the title *Rethinking World History*.

In general *The Rise of the West* was seldom even looked at by my fellow professors of history. Who, after all, can afford to read a book of 829 pages that is not in his or her field? Even Hodgson never said anything to me about it, and the same held true for all my other colleagues at Chicago, with the exceptions of Norman Maclean, who told me it was well written "except for a few sentences," and Gustave von Grunebaum, who once remarked casually as we were walking home together that *The Rise of the West* was "better than it had any right to be," or something to that effect. This was meant as a compliment and probably reflected his realization that I could read only English, French, and German and depended on available translations when trying to understand other peoples. Error arising from reliance on secondary authorities is, indeed, a standing reproach against world history among linguistically expert historians. My response is to point out that specialization invites myopia, which also leads to error. Only close and continual interchanges between historians working on different scales, from the most minute to the most general, can hope to compensate for the defects of each form of scholarship.

Today, thanks to Burke's burrowing through Hodgson's papers, I know that while Hodgson recognized my book as "the first genuine world history ever written," he faulted me for lacking a "basic philosophical underpinning" and for failure to recognize "the development of an overall world-historical configuration as context for particular events."[13] I find these reproaches just, if a bit severe, and wish that Hodgson had survived to read *The Human Web*, my last and final effort (jointly with my son, J. R. McNeill) to put world history into a more adequate philosophical and geographic frame. I wonder what he might have said about it and wonder even more what his own history of the world would have looked like if he had lived to complete it.

Nevertheless, like my rivalry with Stavrianos, the fact that Hodgson and I showed up at the University of Chicago almost simultaneously with such parallel ambitions, and then lived side by side without ever really engaging one another in serious fashion, is a strange coincidence. I used to suppose that if his world history had ever appeared it would rival but not eclipse my own, if only because his prose was so awkward. Perhaps, like Plato and Aristotle, for philosophy in general, we might have jointly pioneered world history as a serious intellectual enterprise. But Hodgson's death while jogging along the streets of Hyde Park at age forty-six cut him off with none of his ambitions realized, while I survived into old age and so was able to continue to seek more adequate conceptualizations of the human story than I achieved in 1954–63.

Three final observations about my magnum opus. I endeavored to proofread *The Rise of the West* carefully, but precision and minute accuracy were never my strengths, and it turned out that the first printings of the book were rife with typos and other trivial errors. I caught some myself, and readers and reviewers pointed others out to me. All are duly entered in a master copy that I still possess. Most mistakes were eliminated in subsequent printings, but I have never checked to make sure that all have been removed. The long list of errata decorating the back endpaper of my master copy is both a humiliation and a reminder of how hard it is to get details straight. Every book I have since published, with only one exception, had at least one typo that leapt out at me during my first fond minutes of inspection. But none ever came close to the forest of petty corrections *The Rise of the West* required.

Overall, it seems to me that what made *The Rise of the West* a landmark book was its demonstration of how different facts, different relationships, different understandings emerge from a global scale of historical inquiry. Simply by looking across boundaries, and exploring compartmentalized historical learning about different parts of the world, previously unsuspected relationships and plausible connections sprang to view. World history as against civilizational or more local national history thus began to emerge, even though my book retained more than a whiff of Eurocentrism, as Hodgson recognized, and did far more justice to Eurasia than to Africa and the pre-Columbian Americas, where the learning available to me was (and remains) far more scrappy.

Lastly, my ambition in writing *The Rise of the West* was greater than reviewers noticed. The title itself was chosen, of course, to invite comparison with Spengler (and Toynbee). It may have been a mistake, since the core message of the book was not that the West was here to stay—as some hasty readers assumed—but rather that since a succession of other civilizations achieved primacy in times past, only to yield pride of place to newcomers, something similar probably lay ahead. Though, as I remarked at the very close, future power-wielders "even if non-Westerners could only do so by utilizing such originally Western traits as industrialism, science and the palliation of power through advocacy of one or another of the democratic political faiths."[14]

But I conceived my book as more than a correction to Spengler and Toynbee. Instead it was intended to be no less than a secular substitute for the Christian worldview. A couplet appearing in the front matter hints at this by bowdlerizing Milton's *Paradise Lost*:

I seek to understand, and if I can
To justify the ways of man to man.

And the book's very first words mimic the Book of Genesis by saying, "In the beginning there is a great darkness." But no one seems to have noticed these literary conceits or recognized the overweening character of my intellectual ambitions.

So much for *The Rise of the West*, its strengths and its weaknesses. Exploring how my ideas continued to evolve in the second half of my life requires a new start.

CHAPTER 3

From *The Rise of the West* to *Plagues and Peoples*

1963–1976

The years between the publication of *The Rise of the West* in 1963 and the appearance of *Plagues and Peoples* in 1976 were in many respects the apex of my career. I became chairman of the Department of History in 1961, nourishing the ambition of expanding the department to embrace the history of every part of the world. President George Beadle and Provost Edward Levi encouraged me in the attempt, and six years later, when I stepped down, the department had almost doubled in numbers. New fields—Indian, Japanese, African, Mexican, and Ottoman history—and new themes—Black history, European intellectual history, social history, and the history of science—accounted for the expansion; and some who joined us were national leaders in their specialties.

But unexpected side effects soon became evident. In particular, the department became too large for responsible self-management. Those voting on appointments and promotions failed to acquaint themselves adequately with what their colleagues were doing in fields other than their own, but voted anyway on slender, and sometimes whimsical, grounds. Frictions multiplied between tenured and non-tenured faculty, and divergent styles of historical sensibility soon provoked faction. Student protest also flared up when we denied tenure to Jesse Lemisch in 1965. An American historian, Lemisch cultivated a circle of student radicals while neglecting the conventional survival tactic of getting something from his Ph.D. thesis into print. But that did not prevent his supporters from charging us with political bias against him.

The next year a similar case in the Sociology Department triggered a prolonged sit-in at the administration building. Fueling these protests was male students' uneasiness at their privileged exemption from the draft at a time when war in Vietnam was dividing the country; and a well-grounded female frustration with traditional obstacles to their professional advancement in academe. These quarrels tore the university community apart as never before. I found it harder and harder to respect the behavior of some of my colleagues, and they got tired of me. So I returned to the privileged life of a professor in 1967 with a sense of relief and some disappointment at the failure of my colleagues to cherish or care for the historical enterprise of the department as a whole.

Four years afterward I became editor of *The Journal of Modern History* (*JMH*). This journal was devoted to European history since 1500 and had been founded in the 1920s as a vehicle for indignant Europeanists who felt they had been ill-treated by the leadership of the American Historical Association. From its inception, professors at Chicago edited the journal, partly because the University of Chicago Press published it and partly because Chicago was a sort of intermediary between insurgent midwesterners, based primarily at Wisconsin, and the eastern establishment that continued to run the

American Historical Association. By the time I took over, the *JMH* had become part of that establishment and a place where young historians were very eager to place learned articles, usually derived from their Ph.D. dissertations, in hope of thus qualifying for tenure.

Submissions far outnumbered available space throughout my editorship, which lasted until 1979, and since criteria for inclusion and exclusion were often arbitrary, I experimented with supplementary forms of publication by filming some additional worthy manuscripts. But that never proved really satisfactory. Commissioning articles for special issues, like one I devoted to Braudel in 1977, meant excluding deserving and desperate assistant professors, for in those years the academic expansion that had run so strongly in the 1960s abruptly reversed itself. As editor I did my best to be open to every sort of historical scholarship and enjoyed reading the scores of articles submitted to the *JMH* and deciding whether to suggest revision, pass them on for external review (and hoped-for approval), or reject them out of hand. This put me in touch with many younger modern European historians throughout the United States and, together with my previous chairmanship of the Department of History at Chicago, incorporated me securely enough into the professional establishment, though less as a world historian than as a (perhaps truant) Europeanist.

Two other extracurricular adventures of these years deserve notice. One is the negotiation that brought Henry Moore's statue *Nuclear Energy* to the Chicago campus in 1967 in celebration of the twenty-fifth anniversary of the first controlled release of energy from uranium atoms. Enrico Fermi had presided over that fateful experiment under a deserted football stand at Stagg Field in December 1942. To dispose of residual radiation, the stand was subsequently torn down, and the site became an eyesore, featuring broken pavement with weeds coming up through the cracks behind a chain wire fence. On the wire hung a bronze notice, originally designed to decorate the doorway to the football stand, telling passersby that this was where the radioactive pile had once stood. One day when walking past the site I was overwhelmed by the contrast between the weeds and rust before my eyes and the monumental celebration of imperial glory that I had witnessed on Vienna's Ringstrasse when visiting that city for the first time the previous summer. I decided that the university ought to do better and began to say so, with the result that I became chairman of a three-man committee to look into the possibility of erecting a commemorative statue and a building to house the reconstituted graphite pile, whose blocks then still existed in storage.

Professor Harold Haydon of the Art Department and the university architect were the other members of the committee. Our adventures in the commercial world of high art are too complicated (and at times farcical) to recount here. Suffice it to say that we soon gave up the idea of reconstituting the original pile under a soaring concrete roof, as projected by the Italian architect Pier Luigi Nervi; we focused instead on a statue to be erected on the exact spot where the pile had stood, inviting Henry Moore to make it for us even though we had no money to pay him. But by happy chance—and it was chance—when the twenty-fifth anniversary came round, the necessary funds were in hand. We even had a suitably designed base on which to place Henry Moore's fourteen-foot bronze statue a few days before the survivors of the original experimental team gathered together to remember what they had done and watch Laura Fermi, now a widow, unveil a statue worthy, in my opinion, of the momentous event it commemorated.

I consider this a real triumph, personally and for the university at large. For Moore's statue embodies the profound ambiguity of the release of nuclear energy—threat and promise wrapped in one—and its aura arouses such awe as to deter even angry protesters from defacing it with painted slogans or the like. The day after its dedication Edward Levi said to me that now the university had a new vulnerability since Moore's statue was sure to become a focus for antinuclear protest and would require police protection. Yet as long as I was on campus and as far as I know to this day, the statue has never been defaced. Instead it has been viewed by thousands of visitors and even become a plaything for neighborhood children, who keep its bottommost orifice shiny by sliding through it.

The University of Chicago was not everything of course. Summer vacations meant family visits with my parents, who had retired to Vermont, and with Elizabeth's aunts in Colebrook, Connecticut. But sometimes we took longer trips. Two were especially noteworthy. In 1966 we flew to Amsterdam, picked up a brand new Peugeot station wagon and set forth to drive through France, Italy, then across the Adriatic by ferry to Greece. There, in preparation for a book I was planning, I returned to six villages—three in the mountains and three in the plains that I had first visited in 1946—to see how they had fared since 1956, when I had looked in on them for a second time. We drove back through Yugoslav Macedonia to Montenegro, then along the Adriatic coast and into Austria, where I saw Salzburg and Vienna for the first time. Next we crossed south Germany to Frankfurt, where I left my wife to continue to Amsterdam, arrange to ship the car to Chicago, and proceed with our four children to England while I flew off to Sofia in Bulgaria and read a paper to a congress of Balkanists.

We reunited in London, traveled to Wales and Manchester to meet some of Elizabeth's relatives, and finally flew to the Hebridean

island of Barra, whence my ancestors once had come, before returning to Chicago, where we soon retrieved our new car. Everywhere I
had the satisfaction of introducing my children to landscapes I had
read about—looking for signs of cultural boundaries, like long acre
fields and the limits of Gothic architecture. The visits to Wales and
Barra constituted family trysts. In Wales we visited a slate mine, still
owned by Elizabeth's family, where skilled workmen were splitting
shingles from blocks of slate, using techniques that had not changed
much since neolithic times. In the village, Welsh indigenes still de-
ferred to English intruders by doffing their caps. I concluded that
we were encountering a rural society only slightly changed since the
eighteenth century, despite being located a mere fifty miles from
Manchester, one of the principal seats of the industrial revolution.

This contrasted sharply with what we had seen in Greece, where
villages were emptying out rapidly as radio and roads suddenly exposed peasants to the seductions of city life, whether in Athens or
in Germany. I reflected that when village poor went off to Manchester in the early days of the industrial revolution, their plight in town
was so desperate that those who remained behind had good reason
to believe their own style of life, however difficult, was preferable.
Hence the stalwart rural conservatism that still prevailed in 1966,
though not for long, since the slate mine closed soon after we had
been there. Indeed the assault of modernity—the Beatles and such—
had already begun to resound in Welsh cottages, as we also saw embodied in the sullen and discontented son of one of Elizabeth's cousins
who belonged to a band that was trying to out-Beatle the Beatles, with
indifferent success.

Visiting Barra was another impressive experience. We arrived in
a small airplane, landing on a beach bared only at low tide, and
promptly met John McNeill, driver of the only car then on the is-

land, who carried my father's name and resembled my cousin Kenneth so closely that it was uncanny. The island had just been electrified for the first time, and the marvel of instantaneous light at night was still fresh in everyone's mind. Seals clustered offshore, fierce west winds, barren hills, and the restored MacNeil castle all were memorable; and after their return, my daughters made a "Barra Book" with drawings, samples of vegetation, and snatches of wool and shells they picked up as we walked about during the three or four days we spent there. Barra, I felt, was a wonderful place to be from—a truly demanding environment that had shaped my ancestors into the high achievers they so conspicuously were.

This trip counts as the high point of family togetherness, and none of us has ever forgotten the host of new experiences and thoughts it aroused. From my point of view, the miracle was that we could afford it. Hotel bills and airfares, even the cost of the new Peugeot station wagon—all were within easy reach, thanks to royalties and the then-almighty dollar. My parents always had to watch costs; we, by some strange chance, could travel across Europe, command the services of hotel staffs, some very elegant indeed, and come back with money to spare.

Two years later in 1968, after my daughters had both left home, the boys came along on another summer trip of less import but memorable in its own way too. We camped for several weeks in Estes and Rocky Mountain National Parks in Colorado, saw a mountain lion and four cubs hunting field mice not far above us, later climbed a glacier to the limits of my strength and breath, then slid down on feet and bottoms. Amateur, perhaps reckless, mountaineering was new to us, and so were the sights of the American wild west—a corn palace in Nebraska, the presidents' heads carved on Mt. Rushmore, the South Dakota Badlands, etc.

Two personal wild-goose chases, taking me to Hong Kong in 1970 and to Soviet Armenia in 1972, were exotic enough to make lasting impressions and seem worth recording here. The invitation to visit Hong Kong came from Professor Noah Fehl, who taught at the Chinese University of Hong Kong. This postwar institution cobbled together two utterly different kinds of refugees from mainland China: a handful of Christian missionaries, of whom Noah Fehl was one, and a few traditional Confucian Chinese scholars. When it came to teaching history, utter disagreement prevailed between the Christian missionaries and the Confucians. When their quarrels grew hot, Fehl resorted to the device of inviting three outsiders—Herbert Butterfield from Cambridge, Cho Yun Hsu from Taiwan, and me from Chicago—to advise the chancellor of the university what to do about teaching history. Since Noah Fehl as well as Cho Yun Hsu held Ph.D. degrees from Chicago, this was a biased panel indeed, and our efforts to find a way to resolve the deadlock were sure to fail, unless or until the administration was prepared to oust the elderly Chinese scholars. They, according to Fehl, should all have retired years before but had evaded statutory retirement by professing not to know when they were born! The two parties no longer even talked to one another, and we only heard Fehl's side of the quarrel. In the end we wrote a report, recommending that bright undergraduates be sent abroad to study for advanced degrees in the Western world and then return to the Chinese University of Hong Kong to develop a historical curriculum that balanced Chinese with world history in a smoother blend than was then possible. I have no idea whether this was done. Our failure to endorse Noah Fehl's cause wholeheartedly severed subsequent connection with him, and the chancellor kept his own counsel.

But Hong Kong in 1970 was an amazing city. As a junior British official remarked to me, it was the only place in the world where nineteenth-century laissez faire still prevailed; and that was, indeed, a good summary. Swarms of poverty-stricken people rubbed shoulders with newly opulent wheelers and dealers, now mostly Chinese but some foreigners as well. Crossing by ferry each day from our hotel to the university campus, I had to pass through a swarm of needy artists trying to sell their paintings to tourists. To my eyes, their mingling of Chinese with Western art traditions was often very successful. I wish I had bought one or two of their paintings; but bargaining was never comfortable for me, and not bargaining presumably meant being gypped. Moreover, I always had an appointment to keep. But I still suspect that some very gifted artists were among that impecunious, anxious crowd.

Our hotel faced directly on the harbor; and the incessant coming and going of ships day and night was as incredible to me as the incessant arrival of airplanes at Chicago's airport. Here was visible evidence of the extraordinary economic upthrust that was later to spread to adjacent parts of mainland China. But new growth was still framed within remnants of the British imperial past. Our hotel, for example, was reserved for whites and a sprinkling of Chinese in Western dress, carefully scrutinized at the entrance by an array of Chinese boys dressed in quasi-military uniforms and backed up, if they elected to question anyone's right to access, by burly guards who kept out of sight most of the time. Altogether the hotel was far more elegant than what I was used to, and like the paintings of the artists at the ferry landing, combined Chinese with European decor and cuisine in very successful fashion indeed.

But all was not well in Hong Kong. Poverty was a seemingly insoluble problem; and cultural encounters did not always result in successful mingling either. For example, one of the side trips I made was to a pleasure garden constructed by a wealthy Chinese business-man whose fortune rested on selling Tiger Balm, a nostrum for al-most every bodily ill. He had there collected an array of Chinese and European art objects, and after his death it was opened to the pub-lic. But, unlike some of the other samples of cultural blending to which I was exposed, this garden, like the History Department of the Chinese University of Hong Kong, exhibited a jarring clash. Na-ked women and other variously repulsive Buddhist and Christian artworks constituted a hodgepodge of bad taste that I have never seen equaled before or since. Obviously, cultural encounters are risky as well as stimulating. All depends on how the blending is done. Hong Kong in 1970, during the two weeks I was there, had plenty of successes and some dismal failures on show.

Years afterward, in 1994, I returned to that city as a guest of Wang Gung-wu, then chancellor of the University of Hong Kong. In 1970 that institution had been a dowdy British transplant, teach-ing the Wars of the Roses to Chinese students simply because they figured in the Oxford syllabus for English history. But by the 1990s the city and the University of Hong Kong were both transformed almost beyond recognition. New high rises sprouted everywhere as a consequence of one of the greatest real estate booms the world has ever known. The Tiger Balm magnate's repulsive pleasure garden was among the casualties, buried under one of the new buildings and long forgotten by those with whom I associated. Poverty had disappeared from public places; the whole city was spic and span, and Western dress was universal. Except for Chinese faces, it could have been any prospering, new-built city in the American South-west.

As for the university, it was flourishing too. Specialization pre-vailed among a talented faculty recruited from near and far by dint of the highest pay scale in the world—or so the chancellor told me. Each expert taught what he pleased, and what each of them wrote and said was aimed at fellow specialists more than at any specifically Chinese or Hong Kong audience. When I was there, the date for the transfer of Hong Kong from British to Chinese sovereignty was close at hand, yet the professors with whom I conversed were confident that they would be able to continue their careers after 1997; their talents were such that employment elsewhere seemed to them merely a matter of applying for vacant posts if they became dissatisfied with their circumstances in Hong Kong. I failed to find out how the Chinese University of Hong Kong was faring. The two institutions were rivals; and the fact that English was the language of instruction at one, while Chinese had displaced the residual missionary heritage at the other, kept them apart.

The most interesting feature of this visit for me was a conversation I had with Chancellor Wang Gung-wu over breakfast. I stayed in his official residence and, since he was soon to retire, asked him what he would do thereafter. He surprised me by saying that Hong Kong real estate was so expensive that he could not afford to stay anywhere in the city after vacating the grandeur of his present quarters. So he expected to return to Australia where he had spent most of his teaching career. Born in Malaya, he and his wife were products of the British imperial impress on a small elite group among their former subjects. Educated in colonial schools, then in Britain, they both had mastered English language and culture as perfectly as any foreigner could ever do. Yet they were also masters of traditional Chinese culture transmitted through their families. The chancellor told me, for instance, that his personal name had been prescribed by a poem one of his ancestors wrote. Its exact wording somehow fixed male names for several generations (was it seven?) within the extended family. That poem was now exhausted, and he, as the best educated of his generation, had just been designated to write another poem that would define male proper names across succeeding generations for another couple of centuries. The task was weighing on him as he spoke, for in this unfamiliar, thoroughly traditional role as family poet, he strove to be worthy of his ancestors.

Binding family tradition about names was familiar enough. My own ancestors, for example, have named eldest sons John-William in alternate generations since the eighteenth century. But we have no written compact—much less a poem—to tell us what to do, and until my own generation the family genealogy had been transmitted orally on dark winter nights in the farm kitchens of Prince Edward Island. But my father in his old age went to very considerable pains to put everything he could verify down on paper, without however prescribing, just describing, how names had been passed down.

What I gathered from my breakfast conversation with the chancellor was that the literate classes of China had resorted to writing far earlier than we, and that family tradition and prescription were considerably more powerful than is common in the United States or elsewhere in the Western world. Here then was an anchor for private, personal life that promised to withstand even the whirlwind of change that had come to Hong Kong—at least among well-educated Chinese families. Mastery of English or any other foreign thought pattern and literary culture did not interfere with a private, Chinese identity as long as family transmission of rules of behavior survived intact. Something similar, I suppose, explains the viability of Jewish and other enduring diasporas. Multiculturalism superimposed upon a core of religious and familial prescriptions for personal behavior surely has a great future in a world as

A Canadian boyhood—
New Year's Day, 1927,
Toronto.

Graduation photo—
University High School,
Chicago, June 1934.

ECHO

The Yearly Newsmagazine

MAN OF THE YEAR
No pussyfooter he
(See PRESS)

Vol. III   Number 1

Man of the Year—University of Chicago Year Book, June 1938.

Battery officer—
Puerto Rico, 1943.

My wife and eldest
child—Chicago, 1949.

Conference on world history—Air Force Academy, Colorado, February 1959.

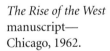

The Rise of the West
manuscript—
Chicago, 1962.

University of Chicago Magazine cover—March 1964.

Siting *Nuclear Energy* under Henry Moore's direction—Chicago, 2 December 1967.

Lecturing on *The Pursuit of Power*—Rensselaer Polytechnic Institute, Troy, New York, October 1983.

(Above) Award of the Erasmus Prize by Prince Willem—Amsterdam, 11 December 1996. *(Below)* Son and father celebrating *The Human Web*—Great Barrington, Massachusetts, October 2002.

tightly connected as ours, and my encounters in Hong Kong brought their reality to my attention as never before.

Another very different and rather more extraordinary encounter with an alien culture came in 1972 when Carl Sagan, once an undergraduate in my Western Civ class at Chicago, invited me to join an American delegation of astronomers and other scientists headed for Soviet Armenia. The organizers hoped to initiate extraterrestrial communication with other high-tech civilizations of the universe. This invitation plunged me into an international world of mathematically adept scientists. Some of them had decided that radio waves traversing astronomical space should be able to connect us with other forms of intelligent life, whose knowledge might be far superior to ours—novices as we surely were in extraterrestrial affairs. Such beings, they assumed, would be able to find ways to communicate with us using fluctuating radio signals. And since mathematics was everywhere the same and the only effectual way to understand and control electromagnetic radiation, it stood to reason that humans could hope and expect to decipher messages beamed in their direction.

My assigned role in this meeting was to estimate the life expectancy of high-tech civilizations capable of generating and receiving electromagnetic radiation. That, after all, was a factor to consider when it came to calculating the likelihood of communicating with other forms of intelligent life—along with probabilities of life and of mathematical intelligence arising elsewhere. Since earth had only recently spawned a single high-tech civilization, I could not provide a plausible guess as to its longevity; but that did not deter Sagan and some of his colleagues—Russian as well as American, with an Englishman, Hungarian, and Czech as middlemen—from making guesses and debating what wavelength was best to use when searching the sky for signals from afar. They figured that other centers of high-tech, already in communication with one another, would wish to greet us by starting to focus radio beams toward earth as soon as they detected such radiation issuing from our planet, which, of course, had begun with Marconi's experiments at the turn of the twentieth century.

Something like half a dozen Nobel laureates had assembled for this occasion, including Francis Crick of DNA fame. When I expressed my skepticism about the feasibility of mathematical communication, Crick told me that I "did not understand the force of the argument for a celestial mathematics common to all high tech civilizations."[1] I was not convinced, and felt the whole discussion carried them into a kind of never-never land. But at the time, and off the cuff, I found myself tongue-tied and failed to defend my view that human mathematics is, like language, arbitrary in its application to external realities and not necessarily and universally true.

Not surprisingly, I was subsequently dropped from the circle of true believers. But I did carry away with me knowledge of the extraordinary fashion in which radio astronomers from around the world communicated with one another, reporting every significant new find by telephone within hours of detecting it. Only a few radio astronomers had access to the necessary arrays of receivers; and all of them knew one other intimately in a professional way across all intervening political and cultural barriers. Yet that did not prevent the extraordinary clannishness dividing the USSR delegation. Armenians consorted freely with Americans and other foreigners, confiding considerable disdain for their Russian colleagues, whereas ethnic Russians kept aloof from us; and Russian Jews mingled with the foreigners even more enthusiastically than our Armenian hosts did. English was the lingua franca for everyone, and toward the close of the conference, it became clear to me that the Americans and the ethnic Russians were fencing with one another when discussing the sort of radio receivers the enterprise might require. Both sides, I concluded, were aiming to get enough information to approach their respective governments with requests for the funding needed to keep up with the other's plans and projects. This, indeed, may well have been the central purpose of those who organized the conference.

Yet meeting where we did, able to look across the border into Turkey and talk with Armenian astronomers about the massacres of 1916, was an eye-opener for me; so were the traces of paleolithic settlements and the ancient forts and ruins we visited nearby. Watching a rural family squat on the doorstep of a church to sacrifice a chicken made another indelible impression. Immemorial antiquity obviously mingled with transnational science and also with nasty environmental damages from new industrial and mining installations, which had disfigured much of the landscape around Byurakan Astrophysical Observatory and the city of Erevan, where we met.

Something of the ethnic tensions within Soviet society became clear to me as well. Overall it was a remarkable experience, not least because of the way some of the scientists exhibited a quasi-religious yearning to make contact with superior intelligence at home among the stars. For they sought, like prophets of old, to contrive anew the delivery of superior wisdom from on high. Both Carl Sagan and his principal mentor, the polymath Philip Morrison, struck me as belonging in that company.

But during all these years my administrative and other ventures were in some sense secondary to my own intellectual undertakings. First, I wanted to convert the broadened vision of the meaningful past as set forth in *The Rise of the West* into a teachable one-year introductory course for college (and high school) students. But instead of replicating the collegial effort that had produced Chicago's Western Civ course so successfully between 1947 and 1954, I decided to undertake the job myself. I was not sure at first whether a satisfactory world history course could be constructed, and none of my colleagues was in the least interested in trying to help me depart from Western Civ as the only proper introduction to the human past. I supposed, naively, that if I could find a way to teach world history to undergraduates, the college faculty and my departmental colleagues would concur that simply because the world was round such a course would be a better way to introduce students to the study of history.

This was a mistake. Years of teaching Western Civ (and in due course a plurality of other civ courses, among which mine was included as an idiosyncratic variant) convinced my colleagues that world history was marginal, dubiously valid, and certainly not a proper substitute for what they were themselves doing to introduce students to the past. So I taught my course for twenty-two years, wrote *A World History* (1967)[2] to serve as a textbook, and, with the help of Jean Sedlar, Schuyler Houser, Marilyn Waldman, and Mitsuko Iriye, supplemented that by publishing twelve small volumes of selected *Readings in World History* (1968–73)[3] and collecting several hundred slides (mostly works of art) for use in class. But when I retired in 1987 world history disappeared with me from the University of Chicago. This was my greatest professional failure, arising from a self-centered effort to do things my own way instead of involving colleagues and assembling a viable world history staff like the one I had helped create for Western Civ during my first years of teaching.

A similar miscalculation blunted the effort to make my personal vision of world history accessible to high school students. World history courses already existed in substantial numbers of American high schools. But most of them only departed from the Western Civ model by interrupting that story from time to time with a potpourri of hurried observations about what was happening elsewhere. The ebb and flow of influences across civilizational lines that I made so much of was largely overlooked, and the centrality of Europe from the time of the ancient Greeks was at least tacitly assumed. But the high school textbook I turned out, *The Ecumene: Story of Humanity* (1973),[4] was a failure, partly because the publisher lost faith in it, but largely because my vocabulary was too difficult for most high school students, and my presentation departed from familiar patterns more radically than teachers were ready to accept. Accordingly, it soon went out of print.

Nonetheless, this text was resurrected by a different textbook publisher, baptized anew as *A History of the Human Community* (1986),[5] and sold to the college market with middling success. Over the years, it yielded larger royalties than any other book I ever published. A sixth edition appeared in 1998, and in 2004 the publisher had not yet discontinued it, though that fate clearly impends since I have not been asked, and do not wish, to revise it yet again. The shorter textbook that I wrote for my own course, *A World History*, also remains in print in a fourth edition, published in 1999.

Overall, therefore, my personal effort to propagate my version of world history was not very successful. Instead, textbooks written by others have become the principal vehicles for spreading world history to American colleges and high schools. Some of them do so in a way reflecting something like my general approach, so my utter failure to establish world history in the college curriculum at Chicago is counterbalanced by satisfaction in seeing how intercommunicating civilizations have come to the fore recently in several successful world history textbooks.

My second intellectual ambition after publishing *The Rise of the West* was to explore the relationship between western and eastern Europe, which had puzzled me at Cornell. Two books resulted, the first of which appeared long before my two world history textbooks came out. The gap between writing a big book and actual publication is always lengthy; and I had already used slack time in the wake of *America, Britain and Russia* to write a little book entitled *Past and Future* (1954).[6] Similarly, in the wake of *The Rise of the West* I wrote a more substantial work, *Europe's Steppe Frontier, 1500–1800* (1964).[7] Let me say a few words about each.

In the spring of 1952, having completed my volume for the "War Time Survey" under A. J. Toynbee's supervision, I had a couple of months of spare time before returning to the United States. The Korean War was then in progress, and the risk that it might ignite World War III seemed very real. Expecting to be mobilized again, and fearing that I might never have a chance to write my big book, I therefore decided to use my unexpected leisure to write a brief, schematic summary of the human past as then apparent to me; I followed that up with a sketch of the current scene, before projecting what I thought the future might bring. I organized the human past around successive eras of communication, distinguished from one another by a series of major technological improvements. This is a scheme still close to my heart.

And I concluded the book by suggesting that some sort of world government was needed to keep the peace, and it would most probably emerge only after another world war. This reaffirmed my prewar belief that contemporary affairs were reenacting age-old political processes, heading toward what Toynbee had called a universal state.

I still think that, given a long enough time, this is a likely pattern for the future of humankind, as the logic of the American world-wide "war on terrorism," launched in 2001, surely suggests. But in 1952 I felt more apocalyptic than I do now, and even though the argument still seems plausible, the indifference with which *Past and Future* was received was only to be expected. The book was too schematic, and too cocksure, to deserve anything else.

Its main importance for me was that in preparing the typescript for publication I was surprised to discover how much I could improve my prose by systematically converting sentences from passive to active voice. This simple editorial device also clarified my own thinking by attaching a definite subject to every verb. This was, I believe, the first time I set out systematically to revise my writing and strive for clarity and conciseness, instead of being satisfied with whatever phrases came first to mind. It is a habit worth cultivating, and, I trust, improved the clarity and grace of all my subsequent publications.

Europe's Steppe Frontier, written in the wake of *The Rise of the West*, was a slender but far more substantial product of my first years of graduate teaching. Having entered the Department of History as successor to Professor Hans Rothfels, I was initially expected to teach courses in German and Hapsburg history, as he had done. The Hapsburg empire, thanks to its complex involvement in Polish, Turkish, and Russian affairs, invited me to investigate the gap between eastern and western Europe that had come to my attention at Cornell. Accordingly, after lecturing for four years on what I called "Danubian and Pontic Europe," I was ready to write and used the spring and summer of 1963 to do so, while awaiting publication of *The Rise of the West*.

My erudition remained modest and drew solely on secondary

authorities. But I asked new questions and, not surprisingly, found new answers. In particular, I applied American notions of a moving frontier to the central and east European landscape. This had already been done by my father's dissertation supervisor, the medievalist James Westfall Thompson, whose *Feudal Germany* treated medieval German colonization beyond the Elbe with nineteenth-century American experience as a silent background presence. I brought the same presence to bear when dealing with later centuries, and recognized three distinct agricultural frontiers converging on European steppelands from north (Russia), south (Turkey), and west (Austria). By emphasizing the advancing tide of commercialized grain farming and the corresponding retreat of the freer and disorderly pastoralist society it displaced, I tried to make sense of a very tangled political history, in which local, quasi-democratic polities—Cossack and Heyduk bands, together with lesser princely governments in Rumania and Transylvania—collided with the Hapsburg, Ottoman, and Muscovite empires. My story ended in 1800, since by then agricultural pioneering was pretty well complete and the old-fashioned, semi-barbarous interstitial polities had all been engulfed by one or another of the three peripheral, bureaucratic, and imperial states.

Most historians, barricaded within one or another national and linguistic tradition, refrain from considering the area as a whole, and the reception of my book was correspondingly tepid. Nonetheless, I regard it as a good piece of work that demonstrates again, on a smaller geographical and temporal scale, the advantages of looking across compartmentalized and ethnically based and biased historiography.

Ten years later, I returned to the theme, this time by sea. The fact was that *Europe's Steppe Frontier* had not addressed important key encounters between eastern and western Europe. These of necessity involved urban and imperial elites, connected by waterways rather than through overland struggles among poor and at least semi-barbarous communities along the steppe frontier. From the start, it was obvious that Venetians were the main intermediaries between Italy and the Ottoman and Muscovite dominions. Accordingly, when I drove with my family from Germany to Greece in 1966, I visited all the principal Venetian sites whose conspicuous traces at Corinth and Nauplion had taken me aback when I first saw them in 1945.

Latent curiosity about seaborne contacts between western and eastern Europe had come back to life for me a year or two previously when a Chicago colleague from the Department of Geography, Chauncy Harris, having just returned from Moscow, entertained his dinner guests by showing us photographic slides from that city. To my amazement, much of the architecture within the Kremlin was unmistakably Italian. How come? Italianate architecture in the heart of Muscovy cried aloud for explanation, since Renaissance influences in Moscow had been wholly omitted from European history as I had previously known it. Accordingly I took advantage of the flexibility of graduate teaching to offer a course in Venetian imperial history for two successive years, 1968–69. My initial ignorance allowed me to profit far more than usual from the handful of students who, in effect, collaborated with me. Then a Guggenheim Fellowship in 1971–72 allowed me to spend time in Greek and Venetian libraries and freed me to begin writing *Venice: The Hinge of Europe, 1081–1797* (1974).[8]

This is a rather more learned essay than its twin, *Europe's Steppe Frontier*, but is also the least successful of my books from an architectonic standpoint, perhaps because I wrote most of it while teaching and could not devote my entire conscious effort to putting it together. The book is consequently rather choppy, and its parts are not as well fitted together as they ought to have been. I must also confess that too many gaps remained in my knowledge and in historical scholarship at large to make it possible to follow the complex cultural configurations and exchanges that went on among Italians, Germans, Turks, and Balkan Christians—both Catholic and Orthodox—as well as Poles, Ukranians, Russians, Jews, Armenians, Bosniak Moslems, and some smaller heterodox religious groups.

As before, this book reached across traditionally separated bodies of learning and explored how competing elites within eastern Europe appropriated aspects of Italian Renaissance learning and technical skills to enlarge their own power and wealth in Ottoman, Ukrainian, and Muscovite society. It has long been conventional to describe changes in the Ottoman empire after the death of Suleiman the Magnificent (1566) as decline. Quite the contrary, I convinced myself that the spread of maize into mountainous terrain, together with commercialization of agriculture in the plains and corresponding increases in urban wealth and skills, kept Ottoman society nearly abreast of the rest of Europe for at least another century.

But costs of these changes in east European societies were also real. Despite all their borrowings, eastern Europeans lagged behind westerners; and it remains true that no one has yet made an adequate appraisal of the intellectual choices made by, and relations among, the ethnically multiplex urban elites of the three empires of eastern Europe between 1500 and 1800. *Venice: The Hinge of Europe* made a stab at doing so, but does not do anything like justice to the theme.

My career as a writer of modern European history concluded with a hasty and much neglected essay, *The Shape of European His-*

tory (1974).[9] I composed this little book initially in response to a request from Professor Sol Tax, then program chairman for the International Congress of Anthropological and Ethnological Sciences that met in 1973. He was looking for an overview of European society to give coherence to a forest of detailed papers; and I was already toying with the idea of writing an essay to point out defects of the historiographical tradition to which I had been apprenticed as a student. In practice this meant composing a personal manifesto explaining what I found defective in the inherited shape of European history, and then sketching in a little more than a hundred pages all the ideas and suggestions about European history that had occurred to me in course of my reading and teaching up to that time. That made for rather crowded pages. Technology, communication, institutions, and ideas all figure in my sketch.

Most of what I wrote still seems very much on target, tying eastern, western, northern, and southern Europe together more closely than national and regional historians are accustomed to doing. But the book attracted scant attention and soon went out of print. Mayhap historians dismissed it as anthropological, while anthropologists dismissed it as historical. Perhaps too, at 176 pages, it was the wrong length for use in classrooms, being too short for a textbook and too long for an assigned reading.

This turned out to be my farewell to European history—the professional niche I had been trained to fill. Looking at *The Shape of European History* thirty years later, it strikes me as provocative enough to deserve a better fate than the oblivion it met. But specialization runs rampant and becomes steadily more multifarious and minute. When specialists write primarily to argue with one another, myopia enlarges its domain; and that has been the predominant trend of historical scholarship in my lifetime. My cast of mind always preferred large views, and, I suppose, that is why this little book and my other two books about European history were so generally disregarded.

A third aspect of my thinking in these years focused on the centrality of population growth and decay in human affairs, and the ecological relations with other life forms that affected those fluctuations. The environmental movement, stimulated by Rachel Carson's *Silent Spring* (1962), played a part in this awakening; so did a splendid book by Roger Mols, *Introduction à la démographie historique des villes d'Europe du XIVe au XVIIIe siècle*,[10] which I discovered while writing *The Rise of the West*. Mols made clear to me how precarious European town life became when epidemic diseases began to circulate more swiftly in late medieval and early modern times, and brought me to realize how dependent urban centers were on immigration from healthier countrysides.

This, in turn, resonated with my intermittent study of contemporary Greece. Ever since 1947 I had been aware that remote, food-deficient mountain villages had sporadically sustained guerrilla warfare in the western Balkans; and for the next thirty years I continued to keep loosely in touch, decade by decade, with the rapid transformation of Greek society by visiting the same six villages I had first called on in 1947. A slender book, *Greece: American Aid in Action* (1957),[11] an article in 1968,[12] and *The Metamorphosis of Greece since World War II* (1978)[13] recorded these visits and my discovery of how new communications, thanks to roads and radio, transformed population dynamics very swiftly, causing peasant numbers first to swell and then to empty out from the villages of Greece.

This dimension of my thought gathered momentum when I decided to follow up one of the loose ends that had come powerfully to my attention when writing *The Rise of the West*. Late in that en-

terprise I convinced myself that an outbreak of smallpox in the Aztec capital was what saved Cortez and his men from having their
hearts cut out atop the great temple of Tenochtitlan in 1521. I said
as much and also jumped to the conclusion that the time when this
dread disease had first reached Europe was probably the second century C.E., with the so-called Antonine Plagues. So I also inserted this
suggestion into a footnote when revising the book. But that was
about all I had to say in *The Rise of the West* about epidemic disease.
Nevertheless, from the moment I recognized its role in Cortez's conquests, I knew that innumerable other encounters between alien
populations throughout civilized history must also have been deeply
affected by differential resistances to infectious diseases.

Accordingly, in 1974, on the strength of a grant from the Macy
Foundation, I spent six months writing *Plagues and Peoples* (1976).[14]
As usual, I brought together what had previously been mutually insu-
lated bodies of learning. On the one hand, there was a rich nineteenth-
century tradition of medical history whose scholars had sifted a vast
array of data on outbreaks of pestilence, hoping to use modern science to identify ancient infections and fit them into prevailing medical terminology. The basic assumption was that disease was a
constant and that mutual adaptation between host and parasite made
no difference. Not surprisingly, that pseudo-scientific enterprise
therefore failed miserably, and the whole effort was given up in the
first decade of the twentieth century, just as epidemiology took shape
and began to develop a new tradition of learning, according to
which parasite and host co-evolve willy-nilly. All I needed to do,
therefore, was to bring a modicum of epidemiological understanding
to the data older scholars had so painstakingly assembled, connect
major outbreaks of pestilence with changes in patterns of communication—already familiar to me from *The Rise of the West*—and

behold, I emerged with a tapestry of new explanations for the persistent phenomenon of civilized expansion. It also became possible to understand why sudden, devastating epidemics like the Antonine Plagues and the Black Death broke out when and where they did.

This book almost wrote itself, as, week by week, grand new vistas of historical understanding dawned upon me. Trying to acquaint myself with contemporary medical and epidemiological learning about the principal diseases that afflicted our species meant exploring the biological and ecological setting within which humankind exists more fully than I had previously done. Alfred Crosby's *The Columbian Exchange: Biological and Cultural Consequences of 1492*[15] was especially helpful in directing me down that path. Thereafter, the ecological frame for every kind of human activity began to loom more largely in my consciousness. That was the central lesson I drew from writing *Plagues and Peoples*. Other historians, especially in France (Emmanuel Le Roy Ladurie, J. N. Biraben), the United States (Sherburne F. Cook and Woodrow Borah, Alfred Crosby, Philip Curtin), and Great Britain (C. D. Darlington, Thomas McKeown), were moving in the same direction, and rather quickly the historical profession at large began to recognize the decisive role that infectious disease played in modern times, killing off vast numbers of Amerindians, aboriginal Australians, Polynesians, and innumerable other previously isolated peoples. My book played a leading part in forwarding this departure, and still constitutes my principal contribution to historical learning at large.

Oddly enough, *Plagues and Peoples* was the first of my books to be rejected by a publisher. Oxford University Press did so on the basis of a negative review of the manuscript from a senior historian of medicine. He emphatically repudiated my resort to inference in the absence of contemporary textual evidence—for him, the only basis for responsible, scientific history. The commercial publisher to whom I next turned was indifferent to truth. The editor's only concern was what would sell. So *Plagues and Peoples* came out bracketed with a history of the Bermuda triangle, where, the author claimed, sailing ships regularly disappeared without a trace! Yet reviewers, most of whom were not professional historians, took kindly to my speculative reconstructions of disease history; and the AIDS epidemic (first identified in 1981) soon began to enhance the resonance of my theme. As a result, sales almost lived up to the publisher's hopes. *Plagues and Peoples* therefore became a real success, even if I like to think of it as only an extended footnote to *The Rise of the West.*

CHAPTER 4

From *Plagues and Peoples* to Retirement
1976–1987

These twelve years saw the apex of my professional reputation but were also a time of diminution as our children left home, ties with the University of Chicago weakened, and my physical and perhaps intellectual energies began to decline. My mother died in Vermont in 1970, and my father followed her five years later while visiting us in Chicago. This closed a chapter of my life. Then in 1979 we sold the handsome house on University Avenue that we had bought from Mrs. Enrico Fermi in 1956. That was where my children grew up: home for them and for my wife and me as nowhere else. There we lived through the tense Black-White confrontations incidental to what was delicately described as neighborhood renewal; there my wife and children wrote and staged annual plays put on by neighborhood children in our basement; there friends and students came to parties and dinners; and there family gatherings had assembled at Christmas and Thanksgiving for twenty-two years. Two trifling burglaries and one hold-up, which occurred almost in front of the house when I was walking home one winter evening, also figure in memories of life on University Avenue. So does the accidental death of my boys' best friend and immediate neighbor in 1977. So all was not sweet, but the apartment on Fifty-sixth Street to which my wife and I moved never became our home. Instead, the white clapboard house in Colebrook, Connecticut, which Elizabeth inherited from her aunt in 1967, took over. Little by little our lives shifted eastward.

One reason was that when the academic boom collapsed in the 1970s, and when mandatory retirement at sixty-five, which had been the rule at Chicago, became illegal, it seemed profoundly unjust to me to hang around with a full professorial salary when younger academics were being dismissed. With the house in Colebrook beckoning, it was easy for me to propose that I taper off my teaching duties to match my physical decline. I therefore surrendered a portion of my salary, beginning in 1977, by going first to two quarters' residence each year and then to a single quarter in 1982. By this arrangement, I would teach exactly as many quarters and receive as much salary as if I had retired at age sixty-five. In the meanwhile, I fondly hoped that the portion of my salary I passed up might rescue a career by supporting an assistant professor. To be sure, I never saw any sign that this actually happened, and discovered ere long that part-time residence drastically diminished my connection with students and, eventually, also with colleagues. Graduated retirement surely matches the gradual decline of one's powers; but it does not fit institutional routine, and from that point of view my experiment was a failure, though, to be fair, it also freed me to undertake a variety of professional junkets and to write some more books and articles.

As my family and professional life at Chicago diminished, outward signs of inward grace multiplied. Honorary degrees began to proliferate, starting in 1974 and continuing irregularly until the 1990s. Most such awards were vacuous, and on one occasion, to judge by the citation, I may have been confused with my father. I never equaled the prestige of his honorary degrees from Edinburgh and Paris. Glasgow was my most prestigious transatlantic award; Swarthmore, the most notable within the United States. My kind of history simply did not impress the major centers of higher learning here at home, even though a fluke made me president of the American Historical Association in 1984–85.

Before that dignity came my way, I had been active on the AHA Council through most of the 1970s and had a good deal to do with relocating the *American Historical Review* to Bloomington, Indiana, as a way to save money for the association by transferring support costs to the University of Indiana. That transaction deprived the managing editor, Nancy Lane, of her job in Washington. A few years later our paths crossed again when she turned down *Plagues and Peoples* for publication by Oxford University Press, New York. She subsequently came to regret that decision and, years later, after handling the publication of my biography of Toynbee, took pains to write me a letter saying how pleased (and surprised) she was at my psychological penetration.

Another interesting assignment from the AHA was contributing a chapter to *The Past Before Us: Contemporary Historical Writing in the United States*, edited by Michael Kammen (1980).[1] This was designed to impress the Fifteenth International Congress of Historical Sciences, which met at Bucharest, Rumania, in 1980. My job was to write about what Americans were doing with modern European history. Helped by five graduate students, I compiled a bibliography of 2,044 books about European history since 1750 that had been reviewed in sixteen English language historical journals between 1968 and 1978. Of these I estimated that between 1,100 and 1,300 had been written by Americans, most of them academics and "products of the great American Ph.D. machine."[2] Conservatism was evident: almost half of the books by American writers dealt with Great Britain, and more than half were political histories. But new themes and new research methods also abounded. My parting judgment was: "Clearly, historians of modern Europe in the United States have been riding the crest of a very powerful wave. Their achievement deserves admiration, which is, for me, rendered particularly poignant by the forebodings I feel about the future of highly specialized work of the sort that has so successfully engaged the profession in the 1970s."[3]

But the book's effort to parade American scholarship before European colleagues at Bucharest fell flat. The French government mounted an exhibit of books that far outclassed ours; and my main profit from attending the Congress was the officially sponsored trip through Transylvania that my wife and I took afterward. This carried us through lovely beech forests on the flanks of the Carpathians to the remains of the Dacian capital that Trajan had destroyed in the second century C.E. It also offered us glimpses of the ethnic palimpsest persisting in Transylvania, despite the best efforts of our official guide to convince us that the population was wholly Rumanian with no remaining trace of Germans or, especially, Hungarians.

In connection with the AHA, I also watched while Hanna Gray presided over a committee that reorganized its administrative structure by instituting Professional, Research, and Teaching Divisions with a vice president in charge of each. Subsequently, I served as the first VP for teaching and made some gestures toward rapprochement with high schools where social studies had pretty well supplanted old-fashioned history courses. Then in 1983–84 my immediate predecessor as president of the AHA, Arthur Link, famous for his exhaustive and pious biography of Woodrow Wilson, made it his business to try to restore history to American high schools by setting up a commission on social studies to inquire into the situation and recommend curricular reform. He initially viewed social studies as the enemy; but actual encounters with high school teachers did something to mollify his rage, and the commission's recommendations, as they eventually emerged, were comparatively mild and completely ineffectual.

I participated in these deliberations and also in three subsequent national efforts to improve the teaching of history in American schools: the so-called Bradley Commission, 1986–93; the National Council for History Education, 1990–94; and the National Council for History Standards, 1992–94. I had become a semi-respectable spokesman for world history, which was still a pariah among most college and university historians. Yet courses called "world history" were often taught in high schools and, in some states, were actually mandated by law! Since the subject was not taught in institutions of higher learning, high school teachers, assigned to teach world history classes, simply had to learn what they could for themselves. They did so usually by staying a few pages ahead of their students in textbooks like the one Stavrianos had written.

These committees and commissions blur together in my memory. All brought university professors of history together with high school teachers and administrators. And it is impossible to tell whether hours of talk and the massive piles of paper we smudged with ink made much difference. The reality of rapid globalization probably had more to do with the propagation of world history in American schools (and more recently also in colleges) than our curricular recommendations, most of which were impossibly ambitious. Personally, I saw how difficult it was to make changes and reach consensus.

I also met some persons I admired among high school teachers and my university colleagues as well. But all the time it took! All the repetitious and irrelevant remarks! After my days as departmental chairman, I had come to realize that my temperament was not suited to academic or any other kind of administration. It was far more agreeable to wrestle with my own thoughts and seek my own answers to questions I found interesting.

All of which meant that as president of the American Historical Association in 1984–85, I made no effort to change anything. My "platform statement" that was circulated with the ballot declared that I, like the later Merovingian kings, aspired to be a "roi fenéant." And so indeed I was, helped by the fact that nothing urgent boiled up within the AHA during my term of office.

I was nominated thanks to a personal connection like the others that had played such critical roles throughout my career. Frances Richardson Keller was a member of the AHA Nominating Committee, representing women and marginalized, part-time junior faculty members who had multiplied after the academic bubble broke in the 1970s. As chairman, I had once helped her when one of my colleagues at Chicago was unjust to her. She contrived to return the favor by persuading the committee to nominate me for the presidency, along with Eugen Weber, a respectably specialized European historian of nineteenth-century France. (Ever since the 1920s, the AHA presidency had alternated between U.S. historians and modern European specialists, so in succession to Arthur Link, it was the Europeanists' turn.) But an election open to historians of every stripe favored anyone who bridged fields. Since my books did indeed range across diverse fields, I attracted more votes and so had the satisfaction of crowning my professional career with a ritual presidential address, delivered in December 1985.

I entitled it "Mythistory, or Truth, Myth, History and Historians," since I wished to challenge deep-rooted professional notions of how to discover and then transcribe historical truth by paraphrasing written texts. Ever since reading Francis Cornford's *Thucydides Mythistoricus*[4] in connection with my M.A. thesis, I had been aware of the close, indeed indissoluble kinship between history and myth. Indeed I find it worth quoting from the "Reflections" section with which I concluded my M.A. thesis to show how my undergraduate philosophical struggles with truth colored my entire career, only to emerge explicitly again in 1985. Here is what I wrote in 1939:

> "Objectivity" and "the facts" have been set up as the ideal for historians in modern times. . . . Great synthesizing conceptions, . . . have been left to philosophers and denied a place in histories. . . . Are we to conclude that insofar as they [Herodotus and Thucydides] permitted their presentation of information to be governed by such ideas, they were not historians, or are we to conclude that insofar as moderns stop short that they are incomplete historians?[5]

In 1985 I was more emphatic, beginning my presidential address by saying:

> Myth and history are close kin inasmuch as both explain how things got to be the way they are by telling some sort of story. But our common parlance reckons myth to be false while history is, or aspires to be, true. . . . But what seems true to one historian will seem false to another, so one historian's truth becomes another's myth, even at the moment of utterance.

My pronunciamento provoked no response—literally. None of my friends or colleagues ever said a word about my presidential address to me afterward. My elder son, who had already started his career as a historian, warned me that I was in danger of developing a private language that would guarantee misunderstanding within the profession. Yet I still consider this essay my most exact and eloquent definition of what the historical profession does and ought to do, for, as I said in closing,

> Unalterable and eternal Truth remains like the Kingdom of Heaven, an eschatological hope. Mythistory is what we actually have—a useful instrument for piloting human groups in their encounters with one another and with the natural environment. To be a truth-seeking mythographer is therefore a high and serious calling, for what a group of people knows and believes about the past channels expectations and affects decisions on which their lives, their fortunes and their sacred honor all depend.[6]

During these years, my long-standing engagement with modern Greece continued, due largely to the fact that I became a member of the Board of the Demos Foundation. This foundation had been established in Chicago by a Greek businessman, orphaned in youth, who put half of his money into it, expecting to use his foundation to set up a school for orphans in Greece. But he died before doing anything to start his school, and the board of trustees decided to use the income from his endowment to help existing charitable organizations in Greece instead. I was initially the only member of the board with firsthand experience of Greece and had the duty of visiting that country each year to decide how to give the Demos money away and check up on how the previous year's gifts had been used. I soon found out how difficult it was to distribute money wisely, and rather quickly I chose to give most of it to American schools already on the ground, whose managers understood about making proposals in writing and reporting afterward, as Greek-managed charitable enterprises most certainly did not. On my advice, the board thus betrayed Mr. Demos's intentions; but I saw no practicable alternative.

An unexpected fallout from my continued activities in Greece came in 1983–85, when a newly established Modern Greek Studies Association asked me to edit their journal. My command of Greek was grossly inadequate, but with my wife's assistance, and safeguarded by a colleague's expert proofreading, we exposed ourselves to judging literary, anthropological, and historical writing about modern Greece and to the tumultuous, politically charged atmosphere of modern Greek scholarship.

Another new engagement was with the *Encyclopedia Britannica* (*EB*). In 1981 I became a member of the board of editors. It met once a year under Mortimer Adler's direction to deliberate about matters of policy. How to organize knowledge, how to revise existing articles, and what new articles to commission were questions I had never before considered; but fundamental disagreement between my view of the all-embracing compass of history and Adler's Aristotelian disdain for the subject meant that my suggestions for recasting *EB* articles were seldom acted upon. Besides, they would have cost too much.

Many of my fellow board members were congenial spirits and I must also confess that the material perquisites—fine dinners and gift copies of the *EB*—were attractive. Membership of the Demos board (administered by the Northern Trust Bank of Chicago) and of the *EB* board of editors in effect gave me a glimpse of the rituals and privileges that prevailed among American business managers— for the *EB* too was a business that prospered until electronic dissemination and retrieval of information undercut its near monopoly as the most authoritative general reference work in English. Thereupon the board of editors ceased to meet without ever being formally disbanded.

Reduced teaching duties at Chicago made travel easier, and I took full advantage of the miscellany of invitations that came my way. Among the more memorable were a walking tour of Mt. Athos in the company of my son in 1975 (from which I dropped out after the first days, exhausted); an extensive tour of western Anatolia in a car provided by the Turkish government, arranged by my Chicago colleague Halil Inalcik in 1977; and a round-the-world trip to Perth, Australia, via Europe, Bombay, and then back via New Zealand, Tahiti, Easter Island, and Peru in 1978. Visiting rather shabby Orthodox monasteries on Mt. Athos, where traditions of entertaining wayfaring travelers were still sustained, was like traveling backward in time; and walking up and down steep hills on rough tracks was a powerful reminder of the obstacles to overland travel that once prevailed. Being chauffeured through western Turkey as a privileged guest of the government was another strange experience. Two things impressed me: the close resemblance in manner and mode of life between Turkish and Greek villagers; and the abundance of ruins from the Roman past, when western Anatolia, before the Antonine Plagues hit home, must have been more densely populated than it has ever been since.

Two academic conferences were odd and surprising enough to deserve mention as well. For both, a geographer, Robert W. Kates of Brown University, played an organizing role, but the first of them,

114

in January 1986, was funded by the Swedish Committee for Future Oriented Research. It brought twenty-two natural and social scientists together for about a week in a manor house near Stockholm to explore "surprising futures." This took place in January, and my first surprise was to find myself in a place where daylight started about ten o'clock in the morning and ended soon after three o'clock in the afternoon. It was an experience I did not relish and that made me wonder, indeed, how people so far north endured so much darkness before electric light. We were divided into three working parties, each asked to propose a surprising future for a different part of the world. My group took on India, and I drafted our report by composing a fanciful tale of the prosperity and power Indians attained after 2047 by applying modern technology to the revision of sacred Hindu traditions while Europe and the "former superpowers, US and USSR" were "effectively paralyzed by internal tensions even more acute than those afflicting Europe."[7] My tale, featuring the career of the founding father of the new India, Mahatma Singh, reads better than more sober efforts at impersonal and quantitative projection that the other groups prepared; but no one, I think, ever supposed our imagined futures were really useful, any more than radio astronomers' efforts to communicate with extraterrestrial intelligence has yet turned out to be. The effort to anticipate surprise was indeed intellectually serious, but the result was trivial.

The next year, a second conference at Clark University, where Kates played a more central role, exposed me to a flood of new data about recent rates of pollution of the earth's atmosphere and hydrosphere. The cumulative force of these reports about old and new chemicals pouring forth from our chimneys and waste pipes convinced me that break points in older ecological equilibria for the earth as a whole were getting uncomfortably close. I departed from this conference with a very much heightened awareness of human-kind's ravages upon our ecological surroundings.

Thinking things over, I emerged with the notion of a three-fold unstable equilibrium at the physico-chemical, biological, and semiological levels, whose overlapping simultaneity and incessant interaction shape our world. Human activity, I came to believe, is governed more by agreed-upon meanings than by external reality, yet the words we use to coordinate behavior are themselves an evolving equilibrium of signs and interact with the biological and physico-chemical equilibria in an inexhaustibly complex fashion to define what actually happens to us and to our terrestrial environment. Such processes, beyond exact measurement or intellectual comprehension, bulk far larger in human affairs, I believed, than conscious purposes or recorded acts. In other words, what our ancestors called God's will or Providence seemed to me a majestic and mysterious process, comprising unstable, interacting equilibria of matter and energy—from electromagnetic fields and quarks to DNA and organisms, and from DNA to ecosystems and societies—culminating in the magic of insubstantial words and symbols capable of coordinating the feelings and actions of millions and even billions of persons, and transforming almost everything around us by doing so.

Finally, visiting appointments at the University of Hawaii in 1980 and at the University of Oxford as Eastman Professor in 1980–81 are worth mentioning. At Hawaii I met colleagues in Chinese and Japanese history (and a gifted graduate student) who revised my understanding of social and economic aspects of East Asian history. I got no comparable intellectual stimulus from my time at Oxford. Indeed, how I was chosen as Eastman Professor remains mysterious; though perhaps it was on the strength of *Plagues and Peoples*, inasmuch as a professor of the history of science did take special note of my presence. But the committee charged with making this appointment obviously did not consult the historians of Balliol College, where Eastman Professors are lodged. Nonetheless, Balliol historians were courteous as well as indifferent. Students however were merely indifferent. Eastman Professors are required to deliver lectures to undergraduates, but since what I had to say did not prepare them for the exams on which an Oxford B.A. depends, they had no reason to listen to me, so stayed away. An audience of half a dozen or fewer persons attended my lectures, and only one retired couple —old friends—listened to all of them. I had never been so dignified, nor so isolated.

I was then finishing *The Pursuit of Power*, investigating the intersection between economic and military affairs; and when I gave a talk at Balliol, claiming that liberal Britain had pioneered the arms race with Germany before World War I, my remarks were received with the same deafening silence that my AHA presidential address was soon to provoke. I should also say that Sir Michael Howard, then newly installed as Regius Professor of History at Oxford, against the wishes of most Oxford historians, was unusually kind to me. He, too, I believe, felt isolated at Oxford. In general, the banter at Oxford high tables, where serious discussion of intellectual and professional questions was systematically avoided, struck me as a step down from what I was accustomed to at Chicago, where serious face-to-face argument was acceptable even among full professors, and where Oxford's style of witty gossip was in short supply.

These and other honors, trips, and conferences played only a small part in changing my mind on what I took to be important questions. Reading books and meeting key figures at work in the macrohistorical enterprise mattered more. Three stand out: Neils

Steensgaard, Immanuel Wallerstein, and Johan Goudsblom. Let me say a word about each.

I do not remember how I stumbled on Neils Steensgaard's doctoral dissertation, *Carracks, Caravans and Companies*, written in English but published obscurely in Denmark. I was enthusiastic, for he explained more clearly than ever before how caravan trade had been organized in Asia and how European trading companies affected older trade patterns in the seventeenth century. Convinced that his work deserved wider readership than it was likely to have in its initial form, I persuaded the University of Chicago Press to reprint it; and with Steensgaard's consent and cooperation, a revised version came out entitled *The Asian Trade Revolution of the Seventeenth Century*.[8] How influential it became I cannot say; but for me it was Steensgaard's portrait of how endowed caravansaries subsidized traveling merchants in Muslim lands, together with a wonderful book by Richard W. Bulliet, *The Camel and the Wheel*,[9] that persuaded me to write an article entitled "The Eccentricity of Wheels," published in the *American Historical Review* (1987).[10] This essay described the divergent patterns of overland transport that prevailed within Eurasia, and emphasized the centrality of caravans and the Muslim institutional arrangements that sustained them. Ever-changing patterns of transport and communication were clearly coming to the fore as I tried to grasp worldwide relationships more clearly than I had been able to do when writing *The Rise of the West*.

My encounter with Immanuel Wallerstein and his concept of a capitalist "World System" pushed in the same direction. I discovered his ideas in 1976 by reviewing the first volume of his masterpiece *The Modern World System: Capitalist Agriculture and the European World Economy in the 16th Century*.[11] I remember being attracted by his analytic descriptions of core, semi-periphery, and periphery, which gave a social-economic definition to the east European societies with which I had dealt in *Europe's Steppe Frontier* and *Venice: The Hinge of Europe*; and I was pleased by the way he made plantation societies in America part of his world system by treating them as comparable to grain-exporting estates in eastern Europe and the Levant.

At the same time, I remained unconvinced by Wallerstein's affection for Kondratieff cycles and was sure that the world system he anatomized had not arisen after 1500, as he assumed. What he did convince me was that financial and economic flows across civilizational boundaries altered social structures and routines of daily life in far-ranging ways. Accordingly, after reading Wallerstein's book, I concluded that a world system (or systems?) reflecting changing patterns of transport and communication, rather than the separate civilizations I had discussed in *The Rise of the West*, offered a better way to understand human history as a whole; and for several years thereafter I experimented with substituting "world system" for the unfamiliar term "ecumene" that I had used previously (in imitation of Toynbee) to describe transcivilizational relationships.

A Dutch sociologist, Johan Goudsblom, was a third and, for me, a much more sympathetic macrohistorian. I met him in 1984 at the Conference on Civilization and the Civilizing Process in Bielefeld, Germany. He, I believe, organized the conference as a way of reintroducing Norbert Elias and his ideas to German academic circles. Elias, after fleeing from Nazi Germany, taught sociology rather obscurely in England during and after the war. By 1984 he was lonely, aged, and long-since retired, and Goudsblom became an advocate for his ideas. None of this I knew at the time. Instead I read a paper on the topic assigned to me, "The Rise of the West as a Long-Term Process,"[12] and had the pleasure of prolonged conversation with

Goudsblom while he drove me to Amsterdam after the conference. We found much in common and I have since continued to correspond with him. Subsequently he wrote a fine book, entitled *Fire and Civilization*,[13] that traces the behavioral changes humans made in the course of their multifarious efforts to use and control fire. This was a novel and important theme whose centrality in human history is still imperfectly recognized, even by experts. Goudsblom, in effect, applied Elias's notions of the "civilizing process" to prehistory and across the entire human past. That was quite a feat, since Elias's own writing was strictly limited to Europe and concentrated on changes in recent centuries. Goudsblom, in short, shared my ambition of studying the whole human adventure and soon enlarged his canvas by pioneering a course at Amsterdam modeled on what David Christian in Sydney, Australia, had already dubbed "Big History," i.e., the history of the universe starting with the big bang and ending with the human career on earth. Goudsblom introduced me to this larger vision of historical reality and in general became a counselor and friend, whose incisive clarity of mind and speech continues to stimulate my own intellectual ventures.

Others whose ideas came to my attention, largely through book reviews I wrote during those years, include Joseph Needham, whose magistral volumes entitled *Science and Civilization in China*[14] opened new vistas on the Chinese past; John Gaddis on the Cold War; E. L. Jones on European economic history; Ester Boserup on population and agricultural change; and Jonathan Spence on the vanished intellectual world of Matteo Ricci, the Jesuit missionary who first won entry into China. Teaching and supervising Ph.D. theses also enlarged my knowledge steadily. Students from whom I learned the most include Stuart Brown, Brian Davies, Robert Finlay, Barton Hacker, Susan Kadlec, Walter McDougall, John Marino, Stephen

Roberts, Hugh Scogin, Jon Sumida, and Marilyn Waldman. And there were others whose dissertations I did not help to supervise who nonetheless contributed to my education by taking part in seminars with me.

Now for a brief appraisal of some of my multifarious publications between 1976 and 1987. The first landmark was *Human Migration: Patterns and Policies*,[15] a collection of papers prepared for a conference organized by the Midwest section of the American Academy of Arts and Sciences jointly with the University of Indiana. Our meeting took place at Robert Owen's then newly reconstructed utopia, New Harmony, Indiana, in 1976. I was the prime mover in proposing the topic. Ruth Adams chose participants and managed the whole affair, which, I felt, went off with unusual success. For we brought together historical, legal, economic, anthropological, sociological, geographical, and theological experts from several countries, whose discrepant vocabularies became obvious. Several participants were even provoked to rethink and revise their papers extensively before eventual publication. The place was eloquent too, and my own contributions—an editor's introduction and an essay, "Human Migration: A Historical Overview"[16]—sum up my thoughts about the costs and gains of migration and the limits of our understanding of the whole process in a manner I still endorse. A fallout from this meeting was that John Voss, executive officer of the academy, took me under his wing and contrived to make me a vice president in charge of nominating new members in the social sciences for a few years afterward.

I returned to the theme of migration again at another conference, this time at Harvard in 1983, and wrote another essay, "Human Migration in Historical Perspective."[17] This is my most perspicacious account of the subject, and it provoked Bernard Bailyn, the reigning expert on immigration into the United States, to ask me where I got my ideas. When I told him they were home grown and derived from general considerations, he was perhaps surprised and presumably disappointed. Good ideas without a shred of evidence from written documents disturb most historians; and my ideas about patterns of migration between town and countryside, core and periphery, were of this character. Like the speculations in *Plagues and Peoples*, these ideas went beyond written evidence, yet I feel confident I was right on average and in most cases.

An earlier example of my penchant for reckless generalization was exhibited at Columbia University in a long-forgotten lecture entitled "On National Frontiers: Ethnic Homogeneity and Pluralism."[18] I took my assigned topic as an occasion to defend one of my oldest ideas: the continued relevancy of polyethnic empire as a plausible future for humankind. The concluding pages of this essay resonate strongly in 2004, when President Bush seems poised to launch a bid for an American world empire by pursuing terrorists to the ends of the earth after attacking Iraq with the full panoply of contemporary U.S. weaponry.

A parallel venture beyond established evidential boundaries was another lecture I gave at Princeton in 1986 entitled "The Conservation of Catastrophe." This too has been published more than once,[19] and provoked professional disquiet rather than assent. This was one of several endowed lectureships I was invited to accept, some of which required publication. The range of topics I chose is evident in the titles of the succession of slender books that resulted: *The Human Condition: An Ecological and Historical View*,[20] *The Great Frontier: Freedom and Hierarchy in Modern Times*,[21] and *Polyethnicity and National Unity in World History*.[22]

The first of these lectures was delivered at Clark University in

1979 and sought to fit history into ecology by treating micro- and macroparasitism as ineluctable dimensions of the human condition. This drastic simplification generalized the message of *Plagues and Peoples* anent microparasitism and the core message of my then forthcoming book *Pursuit of Power* anent macroparasitism. Such reductionism distressed Theo von Laue, the person responsible for inviting me to Clark; but he and George Billias, then chairman of the Clark Department of History, became lasting friends.

The Great Frontier, delivered at Baylor University in Texas, was conceived as a correction to Turner's famous thesis, for I argued that "frontier conditions distorted the social pyramid of European society either by flattening it drastically towards equality and anarchic freedom or, alternatively, steepening the gradient so as to divide frontiersmen between owners and managers on the one hand, and an enslaved, enserfed or debt-coerced workforce on the other."[23] Years before, when I first read Turner's essay, I had been amazed that he did not mention slave labor on the lower Mississippi frontier; and when, in preparation for these lectures, I read Walter Webb's book on what he was the first to call the great (i.e., world-girdling) frontier,[24] I realized that he too had the same lopsided understanding of how scant populations moving into thinly occupied, resource-rich landscapes behaved, despite Russian serfdom, American slavery, and numerous other examples of coerced frontier labor. I still find the view of frontier freedom that prevails among the American public amazing, for of course my little book did nothing to alter the preferred self-image of new men under new skies we have cherished for generations.

My lectures in Toronto were inspired by a similar naughty impulse to upset prevailing pieties. The lectureship honored Donald Creighton, a Canadian historian who had striven throughout life to convince himself and his readers that Canada was becoming a single nation, despite French-English-Indian divergences and the distracting gravitational attraction exercised by the United States. I argued the opposite: that polyethnicity was the mark of civilized society, while ethnic homogeneity was exceptional and largely imaginary. In my own youth I had enthusiastically imbibed Canadian (read *English, Protestant*) patriotism at school in Toronto; and only shed that faith gradually and imperceptibly after moving to Chicago. There of course American patriotism was on offer, but my Canadian past provoked me to resist conversion to belief in American uniqueness and superiority: hence my iconoclasm about the liberating virtues of the frontier; hence my challenge to Canadian efforts to achieve (impose?) nationwide ethnic unity.

As far as I can judge, my Toronto lectures met warmer reception in Canada than my Baylor lectures did in the United States. Canadians, after all, were then trying to come to terms with assertive French separatism in Quebec, and to see it as an expression of civilized norms may have been at least mildly comforting; whereas my message for Americans anent the ambivalence of the frontier was not very new among historians and merely deflating for the public at large. Evidence and mere reason have only limited weight when it comes to shaping national and personal self-images, so these gestures toward upsetting old pieties met the oblivion they invited.

Exactly the same may be said of a lecture I gave at West Point in connection with the country's bicentennial entitled "The American War of Independence in World Perspective."[25] I compared events in North America with Pugachev's contemporary revolt in Russia and with Paoli's rising in Corsica, suggesting that they had much in common. I still think the comparison is valid and even enlightening; but prevailing conviction of our national uniqueness remains proof against such insulting comparisons. Obviously, the fact that I once lamented my fellow historians' energetic efforts to destroy old myths and failure to replace them with more attractive new ones[26] did not prevent me from doing the same thing, inasmuch as the alternative views I had on offer short-changed the sort of collective self-flattery that sustained popular belief in what I set out to challenge.

This was not true of my major intellectual enterprise of these years: writing *The Pursuit of Power: Technology, Armed Force and Society since* A.D. *1000* (1982).[27] I was made aware of the need for writing this book in 1964 when Professor Carroll Quigley, reviewing *The Rise of the West*, remarked that although I had persuasively followed the story of how armed force and weapons technology affected economics and politics in ancient and medieval times, I "unaccountably" lost sight of this theme after 1500. Quigley's reproach struck home. From the moment I read his words, I realized that I had, in fact, forgotten about modern armies and navies, conforming unthinkingly to the nineteenth-century liberal view of the meaningful past that my teachers had passed on to me. According to this version of history, war and preparations for war were an unfortunate heritage from the misguided past and were destined to wither away as rational choices among civilized, free, and self-governing peoples, together with economic interdependence, substituted peaceable negotiation and international organization for irrational and destructive violence.

Obviously, World Wars I and II contradicted such a view; yet when writing *The Rise of the West* I had not had the wit to realize that symbiotic and macroparasitic relationships between professional fighting men and those who supported them remained operative throughout modern as well as ancient and medieval times. By the late

1970s, after decades of teaching modern European diplomatic and political history to graduate and undergraduate students, and after supervising some first-rate Ph.D. dissertations exploring aspects of military organization and technology, I felt ready to take up Quigley's challenge and see what I could do to correct this regrettable defect in *The Rise of the West.* Accordingly, I wrote most of *The Pursuit of Power* in spare time generated by visiting appointments at the University of Hawaii in 1979 and then at Oxford in 1980–81.

My procedure was just as before, bringing what had been isolated traditions of learning into contact with each other. For, with a few outstanding exceptions, European military history had been written as though weapons grew on trees, while economic history, especially the history of the industrial revolution, had been written as though the military market for mass-produced, standardized goods did not exist. Long-standing antipathy between economists and soldiers perhaps explains this anomaly. But after World Wars I and II, when military command and strategic planning interacted so strongly with economic mobilization and deliberate invention of new weapons, it seemed obvious that military, political, and economic history belong together.

Three main ideas emerged from my effort to bridge this gap. One was the proposition that the first modern, market-articulated society arose in Sung China about the year 1000 and, among other things, resulted in the invention and propagation of gunpowder weapons. I owed this insight largely to three splendid essays by Robert Hartwell,[28] formerly a colleague at Chicago, together with Mark Elvin,[29] and most especially Yoshinobu Shiba.[30] Hugh Scogin, then a graduate student at Chicago, also helped me enormously with bibliographical and other guidance. Once Chinese precocity in creating a market economy dawned on me, I made bold to suggest that the familiar rise of towns and of long-distance trade in medieval Europe was best understood as a distant offshoot of far more massive commercialization taking place in China and along the shores of the Indian Ocean. Thanks to the work of several other scholars—E. L. Jones, K. N. Chaudhuri, Andre Gunder Frank, and others—this view has since won wide acceptance, and the reality of a trans-Eurasian market, centered in Sung China between 1000 and 1500 and beyond, is now generally admitted. This readjustment of older views about the unique rise of capitalism in Europe ranks, with the role of infectious disease, as the most palpable change in historical understanding that I ever helped to propagate.

A second new proposition in *The Pursuit of Power* was that close order drill, updated from Roman precedents, made Old Regime European armies surprisingly cheap and remarkably efficient. Drawing on personal experience in basic training, and my close encounter in Hawaii with regular soldiers of the prewar U.S. army, I particularly emphasized the psychological effect of drill in converting poor peasant boys and urban drifters into obedient soldiers, ready to risk life and limb anywhere in the world at the word of command. I am not sure how widely my notion of the psychological impact of drill has been accepted by military and political historians, but at least they did not laugh my claims out of court.

The third main novelty of the book—the proposition that Britain pioneered the contemporary military-industrial complex and institutionalized command invention in the late nineteenth century, with Germany and France tagging close behind—has, however, been received in English historical circles with monumental indifference as far as I can tell. It contradicts a treasured image of British civility and upsets a comfortable habit of blaming the Germans for World

Wars I and II. So the future of that idea is not assured, despite what struck me as very clear evidence. Nonetheless, *The Pursuit of Power* commanded generally favorable attention among my fellow historians, being far closer to their traditional concerns than *Plagues and Peoples* or my books on east-west European linkages.

In general, military historians, a rather beleaguered garrison in American academic circles, reacted warmly to my book. It gave armies and navies far greater weight in pioneering mass production and other generally admired attributes of modernity, including preventive medicine, and was generally respectful toward military professionals. For I claimed that, however destructive their handiwork may be in war, they also made things new quite as effectually as profit-seeking entrepreneurs or politicians and preachers. My own positive experience of the American army between 1941 and 1946 influenced my tone; so did the transformation of the U.S. by World War II. So, like *The Rise of the West*, this extended footnote and correction to it reflects the surge of American power and prosperity that was such a dominating feature of the second half of the twentieth century.

The Pursuit of Power also consolidated a connection with the Air Force Academy in Colorado. That had come my way soon after the academy's foundation in 1954 when those in charge of teaching history to the cadets had to decide how to do so. Oddly enough the first head of the Air Force Academy's new History Department had earned a Ph.D. in church history from Chicago's divinity school, and my father had supervised his thesis. Very likely he was the only air force officer with a Ph.D. in history and of appropriate rank who personnel administrators could find. At any rate, Colonel Sala concluded his twenty-year career in the air force by becoming responsible for deciding what and how to teach history at the new academy.

And since a guiding principle for the whole administration was to depart from West Point's example by bringing academic teaching abreast of civilian standards, he and his colleagues were ready for innovation. Perhaps from the start, or at any rate very quickly, they decided that world history was the way to go. So soon after *The Rise of the West* appeared, I was invited to visit their gleaming new campus at Colorado Springs and give advice. One result was that the academy adopted my textbook *A History of the Human Community* for their basic introductory course. Generations of air force cadets have since been exposed to it, willy-nilly, and it may well be true that the professional officers of the U.S. Air Force now constitute the most influential group of persons affected by my ideas—if indeed they were infectious in the hurried and harried life cadets endured in Colorado as much as at West Point and Annapolis.

Altogether, the last years of my career at Chicago were busy and various. Wider involvement in honorific and advisory roles did not completely choke new efforts to understand the world in general and the human past in particular. My acquaintance with and appreciation of ecological dimensions of human history became more pervasive; focus upon the peasant (and in our time ex-peasant) majority gathered momentum; and, as the phenomenon of decaying urban populations among the rich peoples of the earth became clearer, demographics—both growth and collapse—began to look like a perpetual background phenomenon, underlying and decisively affecting politics.

As always, my ruling idea was that processes, of which contemporaries were often quite unaware, mattered more than purposes. That view of reality gave me license to imagine, to infer, and to make connections that ran far beyond any contemporary written evidence. Cautious, traditional, and "scientific" historians felt otherwise, so generally disregarded what I had to say. Yet, unless I deceive myself, as globalization intensifies and as worldwide processes that no one wants become more evident, the weight of contemporary experience is on my side. If so, self-consciously "scientific" historians, instead of confining themselves to whatever written sources happen to record, will surely have to supplement what they can find in old documents with their own ideas and suppositions, as I think actual historians have always done even without consciously admitting it.

My ideas have become more complex since my student days, but the central thrust for personal and all-embracing understanding remains as strong as ever. I once supposed that everybody was as ambitious; by the time I retired in 1987 I recognized that the public in general and most academics were quite content to live within inherited mind sets. Very likely, the whole effort to construct general truths (read *myths*!) is attempting the impossible. Nobody's ideas last forever, or fit reality exactly, as natural scientists are now well aware. But not to try to make sense of human affairs—no matter how complex they may be—surrenders a fundamental human aspiration. No doubt, trying to do so is not for everyone; but it is nonetheless a proper pursuit for intellectually restless individuals. That has been so ever since the days of Paleolithic shamans, Sumerian priests, Chinese sages, and Greek philosophers and historians. The care and repair of public myths, in short, remains an urgent task for every age, not least our own. And that was what I persistently tried to do.

CHAPTER 5

Retirement in Colebrook
1987–

In March 1987, I retired from the University of Chicago, with forty years of teaching and variegated participation in the university community behind me. The Department of History arranged a farewell dinner at which Hanna Gray, president of the university, spoke briefly. The whole occasion was marred for me by the fact that I knew by then that world history was not going to continue at the University of Chicago. Michael Geyer, a specialist in twentieth-century German history, had been appointed as my successor, so I concluded that a majority of my colleagues were glad to see me and world history depart together.

This may have been unjust. Long afterward I learned that the dean of the college had wished to continue teaching world history, only to meet emphatic veto from Hanna Gray. According to his recollection, she declared, "There is no such thing as world history," and that was that. My colleagues acquiesced, but they had no choice and perhaps were not so distrustful of my work as I supposed when they jettisoned world history at my retirement. But I still regret that the university missed a chance to lead American academia in making world history respectable, as first Columbia and then Chicago had done for courses in Western civilization.

At first, cutting my ties with Chicago did not do much to alter the professional roles I played. Until 1993, the most prominent was membership in the federal government's grandiloquently titled Christopher Columbus Quincentenary Jubilee Commission. This body was appointed, partly by Congress and partly by the White House, to preside over commemoration of the five hundredth anniversary of Columbus's famous voyage. When the commission was set up in 1985, everyone remembered the outburst of national pride expressed at Chicago's Columbian Exposition in 1892–93 and anticipated that something similar would happen again. My appointment actually owed a good deal to the fact that a handful of Chicago businessmen planned to mount a second Columbian world's fair in 1992; but that project soon collapsed when it became apparent that massive clearances of Black housing were part of their plan.

Overall, I was an unlikely member of the commission, being no expert on Columbus and without political connections. John Williams, an officer of the National Endowment for the Humanities and a historian of Appalachia, was the person responsible. Looking ahead to the commemoration, he had invited me and a number of other academics to a meeting in Sante Fe to talk things over. I, of course, emphasized notions set forth in *Plagues and Peoples* about how infectious disease was a critical factor in the encounter between Old and New World peoples, arguing that if this could be made clear to the public it might defuse some of the ethnic tensions that were sure to arise around the celebration. Williams liked that suggestion and persuaded the head of the NEH to nominate me to the White House. Reagan's aides made no objection, so I was duly invited, and arrived at the initial meeting of the commission with no idea of the divergent aspirations that already handicapped it.

For, as constituted, the commission was polarized between persons of Italian descent and Latinos. The Italians saw the quincentenary as an enlargement of their annual Columbus Day observances, which had become an expression of ethnic identity and pride. Latinos, on the other hand, aspired to make the celebration their own but were themselves divided between emphasizing their Amerindian heritage as against their Spanish heritage. Democrats versus Republicans constituted a second rift; and a few individuals with no relevant affiliation, among whom I was one, completed the roster. The White House selected our chairman ahead of time, a Cuban-born Miami businessman named John Goudie. He was swiftly railroaded into office through an uncontested election. Then, to my surprise, I was chosen vice chairman, presumably because I was neither Italian nor Latino and, as a historian, might perhaps know something about what we were celebrating. This was more nearly a real election. I remember being looked over hastily by my fellow commissioners before the vote, and the ambiguity of my name, which might be Irish Catholic or Scots Presbyterian, probably helped to make me acceptable.

But John Goudie was a loner, so the vice chairmanship meant absolutely nothing as long as he was in charge. Under his leadership the commission met quarterly, junketing from city to city within the United States and traveling overseas to Genoa, Spain, Santo Domingo, and the Bahamas. Perquisites were considerable; and some of the places we visited were memorable, especially Santo Domingo and the remote little island in the Bahamas where (perhaps) Columbus first landed. Some of the things Goudie tried to accomplish were admirable. In particular he endorsed the idea of making a lasting mark on the country by endowing Columbus Scholars, to be chosen for their foreign language and historical achievements in high school— one from each congressional district—who would then spend a year overseas to perfect their foreign languages and expand their knowledge of the people concerned. But private donors proved elusive, and the hope of funding such fellowships by profits from a commemorative gold coin proved grotesquely inadequate. Sales were small, partly because the whole celebration went sour, and partly because Congress instructed the mint to issue five other gold coins to support other deserving causes in the same year.

Long before that failure, John Goudie's management of the commission had come a cropper. Nasty quarrels with the Spanish government about who would pay for what handicapped the effort to build a replica of Columbus's *Santa Maria*. Nonetheless, a replica did eventually appear in the international "Tall Ships" regatta and visited several American ports in 1992. What brought Goudie down were rash financial promises he made when launching a trial run of the Columbus Scholars program. This meant arranging for a summer visit to Santo Domingo by scores of deserving American high school students. But when private donors failed to come through, Goudie found himself unable to pay for their housing and maintenance. Variously shady deals with some of his friends and acquaintances who hoped to make money by selling "official" mementoes of the quincentenary also came home to roost. When he resigned in disgrace, I became acting chairman, unable to pay off the commission's debts and charged with somehow winding up the whole sad affair.

Perhaps no one could have made the commission work as had been expected. Old, largely fictitious pieties about Columbus as founder of American greatness withered in the face of bitter attacks on his role in destroying an even more fictitious Amerindian paradise. The angry energy of radical environmentalists, aggrieved Indians, and other Columbus-bashers commanded more attention than cooler efforts to appraise the world-shaking changes his voyages initiated. Thanks to my position on the commission, I was invited to speak on a great many campuses about how to understand the quincentenary; but my efforts to defend the historical importance of Columbus's voyages counted for little. I was indeed ill prepared to meet such an angry man as Kirkpatrick Sale, whose book *The Conquest of Paradise: Christopher Columbus and the Columbian Legacy*[1] was the most scholarly, eloquent, and wrong-headed attack on Columbus that the quincentenary provoked. Sale had done his homework with skill and panache, combing through details of Columbus's life to show how he violated twentieth-century environmental and humane proprieties. But when the John Carter Brown Library asked me to debate him head to head, I came away feeling that I had not been able to countervail the historical injustice of Sale's denunciation. He measured Columbus by standards imported from our own time; but what historian does not do something similar? And my effort to subordinate Columbus's actions, and everyone else's, to an impersonal, world-changing ecological collision demoted human purposes and personalities from the center of attention in a way most people found unattractive, however plausible it might be.

Public TV and the Boston station WGBH provided me with a better chance to present my notions about the biological dimension of the Columbian encounter to the American public. The station produced an ambitious series of eight half-hour programs entitled *Columbus and the Age of Discovery*. Ahead of time, the producers invited me to consult with them on what to say and how to say it. They and everyone else concerned were genuinely interested in historical accuracy, and I persuaded them of the importance of infectious disease in destroying Indian cultures and populations. But they also wanted to be eye-catching and encrusted their films with what I came to think of as "visual rhetoric," gathered rather indiscriminately from contemporary rural Mexico. Nevertheless, these films were widely exhibited and became the principal vehicle for propagating my ideas about what mattered most about the quincentennial.

Overall my experience with the commission was disappointing. The diverse personalities that Congress and the White House had thrown together in constituting it never jelled into a coherent body. No one foresaw the storm of criticism the quincentenary provoked, and no one found an effective response. Instead ethnic and a few key personal rivalries prevailed within the commission; while Goudie's solo effort to raise large sums of money from the private sector uniformly failed. Our brush with the legislative process when arranging for issuance of a commemorative coin turned out to be both tedious and clumsy, and our one good idea—the Columbus Scholars program—died aborning.

Another disappointing experience for me was a semester of teaching at Williams College in the spring of 1988. Williams is a top-notch college, and the students who showed up in my classes were capable but uninterested. I undertook to teach the history of Islam, which was conspicuously absent from the Williams curriculum, and chose Marshall Hodgson's *Venture of Islam* as a textbook. This was a mistake since it was too long to be read in its entirety and too clumsily written to command my students' attention. I expected them to read fifty pages a week and discuss in class what Hodgson had to say. But after weeks of lame discussion punctuated by awkward silences, one weary student explained to me that he could not read fifty pages a week because he practiced lacrosse all afternoon and was too exhausted to read at night. Multiple teams in multiple sports meant that almost all Williams undergraduates were similarly engaged every weekday afternoon, and habitually used their weekends to catch up on classroom assignments. They wrote good papers and knew how to cram for an exam; but class discussion was unfamiliar and unwelcome. After all, they were preparing to enter the American workforce at the top—Wall Street and the like. Exploring the strange, unfamiliar world of Islam seemed irrelevant to them. My fiasco at Williams made me realize how privileged I had been at Chicago, where intellectual ambition among undergraduates was the norm and sports were always subordinate.

A second seminar at Williams was devoted to *The Rise of the West*. I assigned one chapter of the book to each participant, each of whom I asked to make a presentation in class about its strengths and weaknesses. But this, too, was a failure. They knew too little to do the job well and were probably inhibited by fears that I would resent negative remarks. Nonetheless, this seminar did bear fruit in the form of an essay I wrote when it was over, "*The Rise of the West* after Twenty-five Years," and published in the initial issue of the *Journal of World History* (1990).[2] I had not read my own book through from cover to cover since its publication and found much to be pleased with as well as some serious flaws. Without the stimulus of the Williams seminar I would not have had occasion to reassess my book, and subsequent printings of *The Rise of the West* would not have carried that essay as a preface.

Nonetheless, I concluded from my experience at Williams that trying to teach even gifted and well-trained undergraduates was not my forte, and declined subsequent invitations that came my way. My father, by contrast, had become an itinerant teacher for almost two decades after his retirement. He needed the extra money and found access to colleagues and a library a welcome relief from rural isolation. But my retirement annuities and royalties actually exceeded my income as an active professor; and a series of conferences and lecture invitations, together with extended visits to libraries in connection with books I was working on, provided me with the sort of collegial support my father had sought as a teacher. As in many other ways, the expansion of academic resources that occurred in my lifetime made my years of retirement far easier and more comfortable than my father's had been.

Until 1996, when my career reached its public apex with the award of the Erasmus Prize, interesting engagements came along year after year. One of these was my connection with the World History Association (WHA). It was founded in 1984 in Colorado, with critical support from Air Force Academy historians, and swiftly became the organizing focus for world history in the whole country. WHA brought high school teachers together with university historians, and since high schools were where world history was taught—at least to begin with—a handful of dedicated high school teachers, of whom Heidi Roupp from Aspen, Colorado, was the chief, played leading roles from the start. Affiliation with the American Historical Association soon permitted the WHA to arrange sessions at AHA annual meetings, and rather quickly, foreign members and affiliated organizations joined in, especially from Asian countries. Above all, after 1990, when the *Journal of World History* began to appear under Jerry Bentley's editorship, it quickly attracted high-quality contributions from all over the English-speaking world and beyond. I had only a very marginal part in all this but was often consulted, and regularly I cheered everyone on, while their very substantial and sustained successes cheered me.

The year 1990 was notable in three other ways. In that year lectures I had delivered at the University of Virginia in 1989 were published under the title *Population and Politics since 1750.* In preparation I spent a few months at the Woodrow Wilson Center in Washington and used the Library of Congress for the first time to sharpen "my thoughts about the demographic diapason that, like the drones of the bagpipe, sets a background tone against which the shriller voices of political debate compete for attention."[3] These lectures sum up my notions about how rising and shrinking populations lay behind the rapid political and economic changes of recent centuries—a theme that dated back to my Ph.D. thesis and to my observation of Greek villages after 1944. The resulting essay, though adequate on Europe, is weak on extra-European responses to population growth, and my discussion of the politics of declining populations is even sketchier, though provocative and plausible enough.

The year 1990 was also when I reviewed a book by Ernest Gellner, *Plow, Sword and Book: The Structure of Human History.*[4] Though I rejected his view that the industrial mutation of Britain in the eighteenth century was a miracle, his discussion of language and the social role it plays among human beings struck home to me. In fact, Gellner finally answered the haunting question "What is Truth?" that I had abandoned when my essay on the subject fell into hopeless confusion at Cornell in 1940. This enlightenment constitutes a sort of capstone for my entire intellectual endeavor, and I feel correspondingly grateful to him.

Born in Czechoslovakia, Gellner was educated in England as a philosopher and anthropologist and did fieldwork in Moroccan villages, paying special attention to variant local forms of Islamic belief and practice. Like my Chicago mentor Robert Redfield in the 1930s, Gellner aspired to generality and was especially interested in words and ideas as regulators of human behavior. What I took from his pages in 1990 was the view that language was primarily an instrument for sustaining social cohesion and cooperative action. Agreed-upon meanings were what mattered. Whether such meanings corresponded to external reality remained secondary and was often irrelevant, since by acting as if it were so, people could achieve their ends and, in a sense, create what they believed in—e.g., religious institutions, political states, or whatever else they imagined to exist.

In short, words and languages were largely autonomous systems, operating with only sporadic constraints from outside. Acting together was critical. That was what promoted group survival and avoided paralyzing quarrels. Humans, of course, had to find enough food to sustain life; and innovations that enlarged their access to energy flows, like control of fire, the bow and arrow, or steam engines, always tended to spread. But until very recently, technological innovation had little or no connection with revered truths. Such truths were what worked, conducing to collective survival by telling everyone how to behave and cooperate in all ordinary circumstances. The way mathematical and experimental science in Europe began to influence, even to guide, technological invention in the latter nineteenth century was something new under the sun, according to Gellner, and was perhaps of only limited viability among humans who continued to need vibrant, emotionally sustaining beliefs to make their individual and collective lives worth living.

An essay I wrote for Martin Marty, entitled "Fundamentalism and the World of the 1990s,"[5] coincided with and in part reflected my encounter with Gellner's discussion of social truth. His ideas had been largely shaped by his study of how local forms of Islamic belief in Morocco actually operated. My essay attempted to sum up and interpret studies of diverse local "fundamentalisms" that Marty had commissioned as part of a large-scale study. Accordingly, my speculations about how refurbished religious beliefs might assist painful changes incident to the breakup of age-old village communities combined a new appreciation of the critical role of agreed-upon meanings, derived from Gellner, with long-standing notions about the worldwide disruption of village communities. This essay, too, summed up a central theme of my thinking about contemporary affairs, acknowledging the apparent retreat, perhaps decay, of my own naturalistic view of the human condition.

That same year inaugurated two other vivacious connections. One took me to São Paulo, Brazil, where in 1988 an American journalist, Norman Gall, had set up what he called the Fernand Braudel Institute of World Economics. It sought to disseminate better understanding of strategies for what economists and others commonly referred to as "development," in Brazil and other countries of Latin America. In 1991, Gall brought together a group comprising (with others less conspicuous) a youthful Harvard economist, Jeffrey Sachs, then confident of exactly how to cure faltering east European economies by straightforward fiscal action; a slightly more youthful Russian, Grigori Yavlinski, then active on the fringes of national politics; and myself, an aged skeptic of quick fixes for social ills. We were asked to discuss similarities and differences between the situation in eastern Europe and in Latin America.

Our wisdom was dubious; but my encounter with Yavlinski was among the most surprising of my life. He spoke English rather fluently, having studied it privately when, as a sergeant in the Red Army, he became entranced by the free-market economic ideas set forth by American economists. That was unusual enough and was magnified by the fact that he had first attained fame (and privileged leisure) by becoming heavyweight boxing champion of the Red Army. His strength was phenomenal, though his physical condition in 1991 was in obvious decay. But when Gorbachev inaugurated *perestroika* and *glasnost,* Yavlinski had been ready with his radical, imported American ideas and had rocketed to public attention by circulating a short paper about how to make the Soviet Union over into a market economy instantaneously, or almost so. When I asked about his background, he told me that he did not know whether he was of Ukrainian, Russian, or Jewish descent. His father, an orphan of World War I, knew absolutely nothing of his parents; the name Yavlinski was ambiguous and perhaps inauthentic. So here was a man in a prominent and perhaps influential position with no known family history and with ideas that, likewise, were rootless, abstract, and entirely unhistorical. When I observed that free markets in Russia would likely generate ethnic frictions because Armenians and Jews were far better prepared to take advantage of the market than others, this was an entirely new thought for him. Yet he was then head of a small political party in Russia, and kept in touch with his supporters by phone every day!

Sachs's ideas were as universal and almost as unhistorical as Yavlinski's, but he was intrigued by my suggestion that a market in competitive gift-giving (read *corruption* and/or *political contributions?*) coexisted with, and often countervailed, price competition as a way of allocating resources in fully "developed" lands like the United States and western Europe as well as in Russia and Brazil. He even promised to think about it, but we failed to keep in touch subsequently, so I do not suppose he has ever had time to do so.

For a little longer than a week, our traveling circus performed in several far-flung Brazilian cities, some of which I had never even heard of before. This showed me the magnitude and variety of the country, its vast resources together with acute problems arising from massive urban in-migration, tense race relations, and sharp income inequality. Gall also brought me to Brazil a second time in 1994, for another, but less memorable, conference. These brief exposures left me generally ignorant but nonetheless impressed by the country's size and complexity and by Norman Gall's missionary effort to propagate North American notions among a few privileged Brazilians.

A second new engagement, also dating from 1990, was with Armand Clesse, director of the Luxembourg Institute for European and International Studies. The government of Luxembourg had founded this institute after World War II as a surrogate for creating a full-blown university, and by the time Clesse began to invite me to attend the institute's conferences, he had defined an overarching theme, "The Vitality of Nations," and chose the Harvard Faculty Club as the seat for most of his meetings. His preferred format was to circulate a book manuscript or shorter essay ahead of time and invite participants to discuss the text for two days in the presence of the author, who was expected to respond to criticism and suggestions as they arose. Clesse gathered about twenty distinguished economic historians, sociologists, and social theorists from Europe and the United States for these occasions. Everyone spoke English fluently, so discussion was lively and I much enjoyed the give and take of argument with persons like David Landes, Charles Kindelberger, Randall Collins, Johan Goudsblom, and others.

As so often, I felt that the discourse of economists and economic historians was too narrowly conceived, neglecting fundamental dimensions of human affairs by assuming stable and uniform "human nature" where in fact swift change prevailed. Accordingly in 1996 I wrote a paper entitled "The Disruption of Traditional Forms of Nurture" for discussion at a conference held, this time, in Luxembourg itself. My paper sketched what I took to be the breakdown of traditional forms of village life and nurture that set in around the world after World War II. This, I argued, called into question not only the "vitality of nations" but also the local continuity of human societies and cultures everywhere. Discussion was lively as usual; my colleagues were skeptical and corrected some details; but I felt no need for more than a few adjustments before releasing my paper for publication, along with a transcript of the discussion it provoked.[6]

This enterprise, in effect, summed up my investigations of village and rural life. Most American historians of my generation have little or no personal acquaintance with the realities of old-fashioned farming. Mine is superficial and an outsider's view; but all the same I believe it did allow me to notice and give more nearly proper weight to the experience of the human majority across historic time. "The Disruption of Traditional Forms of Nurture" remains my best effort to explain the rural basis of civilized society and how twentieth-century communications, together with unprecedented population growth, made the traditional, parasitic relationship between cities and villages unsustainable.

I remain convinced that the peasant and ex-peasant majority matters in world affairs and that finding a new accommodation between rural and urban segments of society constitutes the most fundamental human agendum of the twenty-first century. The American style of large-scale, high-energy mechanized farming that has swept across North America and several other regions of the earth since the 1930s is an unlikely candidate for a sustainable worldwide pattern; but viable long-range alternatives remain hard to discern. Nonetheless, however unsuccessful I may have been in changing anyone's mind, my association with Armand Clesse and participation in the conferences he organized year after year were a recurrent delight for me.

Three other conferences brought new ideas to my attention or clarified older notions. Let me list them chronologically, beginning with a trip to Tromso, Norway, in the summer of 1993 under the aegis of the Norwegian Nobel Institute. The occasion was a conference, "The Fall of Great Powers," that Geir Lundestad, the institute's presiding officer, managed with particular grace and skill. Traveling north of the Arctic Circle, and catching cod in a Norwegian fjord by jigging from shipboard with a bare hook, was extraordinary in itself. The company was good—Paul Kennedy, Wang Gung-wu, Wolfgang Mommsen, Alec Nove, and others—and my own "Introductory Historical Commentary"[7] sharpened many of the ideas that had preoccupied me for decades: polyethnic empire versus nation state, demography and migration, nurture of the young, human need for personal identification within primary communities, and the role of religious faiths—whether revealed or secular—in sustaining urban societies and public order, etc. Like the essay on nurture, this is among the best efforts I ever made to think big and see clearly what mattered most in human affairs.

Then in 1994 John Gaddis invited me to attend a conference he organized in Athens, Ohio, on "Chaos Theory and History." Previously, I had been unaware of this branch of mathematics, and came away intrigued but unconvinced of its helpfulness for historians. Chaos and spontaneous pattern formation are all very well and probably do describe some dimensions of human experience; but self-awareness and the overriding role of language in affecting human actions seem recalcitrant to chaotic patterns. Soon after, in 1996, I was invited to join the Santa Fe Institute as a member of their research board. Murray Gell-Mann and other leading lights of the institute were then planning to expand their biological and other scientific inquiries into the field of human history, and I suppose I was the most obvious person who pretended to acquaintance with the human past as a whole. For the next few years I attended annual meetings and witnessed presentations of computer program results about the spontaneous emergence of complexity and new kinds of behavior among dots and crosses on a computer screen and the like. Prevailing ideas about how life had emerged from inorganic matter were indeed plausible; efforts to illuminate the emergence of markets and how markets changed human behavior were less persuasive; and I eventually resigned from the board because I felt that I understood too little and had nothing to contribute to their computer-based efforts to make human affairs intelligible.

Maybe I was too old to adjust my habits of mind. Maybe, as Francis Crick had said to me in Armenia, I just don't understand mathematics. Or maybe the precision of computer quantification reveals the inadequacy of verbal and of quantitative discourse to address reality. At any rate, as far as I can tell, neither chaos theory nor computer models have yet been able to further understanding of human history in any significant way. Quite the contrary, these brief flirtations with imperially minded scientists, seeking to bring human history into their mathematical domain, convinced me instead that the natural world and human science were both in fact part of historians' proper domain. It seemed clear to me that evolving physical nature, evolving life forms, evolving human meanings, and coordinated human action based on such meanings constituted a seamless whole. An initial level of complexity permitted the emergence of ever more energy-profligate higher complexities, and the result was a universe and planet earth where astounding and extraordinary intricacy prevailed. My notion of a three-fold unstable equilibrium—physico-chemical, biological, and human semiotic, united into one by energy flows—still seemed plausible and remained the best I could do to make sense of the whole grand evolutionary process.

When in November 1996 I was invited to Amsterdam to receive the Erasmus Prize, this was the message I sought to attach to my new dignity. That prize was the greatest honor I ever received and one I scarcely deserved. Since 1958 it has been awarded annually for distinguished contributions to "culture, society or the study of society . . . of outstanding importance for Europe."[8] Funded by the Dutch government and administered by an independent foundation, the prize is named for Erasmus, the Dutch humanist and biblical scholar who did all he could to reform the Christian church and preserve the unity of European society at the time of the Reformation.

To receive an award so named was unusually resonant for me inasmuch as my father, best known as a Calvin scholar, made Erasmus into something like his personal patron saint. He kept a copy of Holbein's portrait of Erasmus on his desk and identified his own irenic views about the folly of theological quarrels with those of Erasmus. All of which meant that receiving the Erasmus Prize constituted a new and unexpected bond with my father twenty-one years after his death.

Attaining such an honor was indeed surprising. The foundation in charge decides each year in what general field of endeavor to award the prize, and in my year "the study of society" was chosen. A committee of Dutch scholars, among whom Johan Goudsblom was one, were asked to make nominations, and, largely I believe at his instigation, my name was chosen. Only one historian had won the prize before me: a Swiss named Werner Kaegi, best known for a seven-volume biography of his fellow citizen Jacob Burckhardt. That kind of detailed history could hardly have been more different from mine; and I had the further oddity of being the first Erasmus Prize winner who did not live in Europe. The list included politicians like

Robert Schuman and Jean Monnet; artists like Marc Chagall and Henry Moore; as well as filmmaker Charlie Chaplin; a theologian, Martin Buber; and an anthropologist, Claude Levi-Strauss. Perhaps because choices are so varied, the prize has never been much noticed outside of the Netherlands, and the foundation's hope of rivaling the prestige of Nobel Prizes has fallen far short. Choosing me—a comparative unknown in European intellectual circles—assuredly added nothing to its prestige and added little to mine in the United States, where the prize is, for all practical purposes, unknown.

All the same, meeting and conversing with Queen Beatrix, who proved to be a ready conversationalist; bending my neck to Prince Willem Alexander to receive a riband and parchment from his hands; and acknowledging the honor they had paid me with a few words afterward was a deeply gratifying ceremonial apex for my career. Two lectures I delivered in connection with the prize, the quasi-autobiographical "Reshaping the Human Past" and the more impersonal "Changing World Views,"[9] set forth how I had begun to view the intellectual history of the twentieth century as the emergence of an evolutionary, i.e., historical, synthesis of all the sciences. Four years later, I elaborated on the same theme before an American audience in Texas, and this time my thoughts were published in part as "A Short History of Humanity" (2000)[10] in the *New York Review of Books*, and in full in *History and Theory*, where I had by then joined that journal's editorial committee.[11]

Running around to conferences and writing articles and book reviews did not take all my time. But the first four books I wrote during my retirement, *Arnold Toynbee: A Life* (1989),[12] *Hutchins' University: A Memoir of the University of Chicago, 1929–1959* (1991),[13] *Colebrook: An Historical Sketch* (1996),[14] and *Grandfather Stories*

(1996)[15] added little to my stock of ideas, other than spelling out what I remembered and discovered about environments and personalities that helped to shape my mind. I have already mentioned the painful diminution Toynbee and Hutchins suffered in my estimation when I examined their careers retrospectively. Finding that giants of my youth had feet of clay was disappointing; finding that New England town meetings were not democratic, even (or especially) in pioneer times, was another disillusionment. Only by venturing into family history, where written records were lacking and my personal memory could not be checked, did I find undiminished and untarnished heroes. Recognizing how admirable my parents and my McNeill grandparents in Prince Edward Island had been, and realizing how very much I owed to them, perhaps helped to countervail the lessened stature that Toynbee and Hutchins came to occupy in my estimation. But I wonder what fuller documentation and more accurate knowledge of my ancestors' lives would reveal? As things stand, ignorance derived from selective oral transmission of family history is comforting. Blessed, mayhap, are the ignorant? Or were my ancestors really able to work and labor throughout their lives, admired by those around them, and unmarred by personal faltering and failure? Who can say for sure?

During these same years I also found time to elaborate some of my most fanciful and fundamental notions by writing *Keeping Together in Time: Dance and Drill in Human History* (1995).[16] This book enlarged upon a theme in *The Pursuit of Power*, where I had argued that European soldiers in the seventeenth century, through oft-repeated drill, forged new collective identities as a result of what I came to call "muscular bonding." This idea was, in turn, a fallout from my own response to close order drill in 1941, whose pointlessness did not prevent me and my fellow draftees from experiencing a mild euphoria when strutting around a dusty drill field at the word of command, keeping in step and every so often sounding off with "Hut, hup, hip, four," shouted in unison. That surprised me at the time, since it was a hot and sweaty as well as senseless pastime. I surmised that we were perhaps inadvertently echoing practices of Paleolithic predecessors who had danced before and after successful hunts, mimicking what they had done and were about to do, and thereby strengthened cooperation and heightened individual courage through ritualized rhythmic exertion. But in *The Pursuit of Power* I compared the new forms of drill that Maurice of Orange introduced into the Dutch army with classical Greek and Roman practices, and let it go at that.

Nonetheless, I was aware that if military drill had such powerful psychological effects as I believed, the phenomenon of muscular bonding had to be a general human experience, and its expression could not be confined to a few centuries in European history. An invitation to deliver the Lee Knowles lectures on military history at Trinity College, Cambridge, in 1992 triggered an initial effort to investigate the question across the whole spectrum of the human past. But by concentrating on military examples, I missed the centrality of ordinary festival dancing and left out voicing as well.

I quickly discovered some of my deficiencies, when, immediately after delivering my lectures at Cambridge (where my audience had been frostily indifferent to what I had to say), Johan Goudsblom invited me to Amsterdam and assembled a group of colleagues to listen to a summary of what I had said. The Dutch were both interested and critical, pointing out how lopsided my approach had been, and how much I did not know about human evolution. Obviously, more work was needed to make my hypotheses convincing.

Accordingly, in the following year, I made a prolonged visit to

Washington, where the librarian of Congress, James Billington, offered me privileged access to the library he presides over. There I explored human evolution, chimpanzee behavior, and religious expressions of dance and trance more fully than before. Subsequent short visits to the libraries of Yale and Wesleyan Universities filled in some remaining gaps; but the final text of *Keeping Together in Time* continued to reflect deficiencies of my inquiries, since the chapter on politics and war is far more firmly grounded in fact and scholarship than those on human evolution, small community festivals, and religious ceremonies. In addition, soon after its publication, correspondence with two musicians convinced me that I had underplayed the emotional impact of voicing and music in writing about muscular bonding.

Throughout my work on this book, I was haunted by the nearly total lack of written evidence for what I was arguing. Emotions so vague and diffuse as those aroused by keeping together in time are simply not talked of, much less written about. Nor could I discover any scientific discussion of the emotional impact of marching and dancing. Yet a warm sense of solidarity with one's fellows, however inarticulate it remained, became, I believed, an essential prop for proto-human societies. It allowed them to sustain cooperation while growing in size far beyond the limits modern chimpanzee bands attain; and such enlarged proto-human bands in turn became the setting within which grammatical language, agreed-upon meanings, and the ability to shift attention back and forth between present, past, and future all dawned, making apelike talkers into fully human beings for the first time. But how speculative it all remained! And how important if true!

I had a rude reminder of the fragility of my argument when I submitted my manuscript to the University of Chicago Press, and a biologist on the press board took violent exception to my remarks about warm emotional responses to military drill and, being a man who had hated drill, accused me of intellectual irresponsibility. The editors at the press dillydallied, proposing further reviews of my manuscript. I felt they should have been more confident of the quality of my work, so withdrew it and was at least mildly vindicated when faculty reviewers for Harvard University Press accepted it without cavil. Still, this was one more break with Chicago, and hurt far more than the rejection my much less speculative *Plagues and Peoples* had suffered from Oxford University Press twenty years before.

For despite the speculative recklessness and deficient research behind this book, I feel sure I was right in essentials and that muscular bonding was and remains an important undergirding for human groups of every description. Believing that I now understood this level of human communication and its role as a propaedeutic for fully articulate and grammatical speech (combined with the new understanding of how speech sustains social cohesion and cooperation that I had drawn from Ernest Gellner) brought my ideas about human uniqueness and our historical trajectory together in a far clearer way than ever before. World history, with which I had been preoccupied for more than fifty years, began to jell around the notion of communication nets, sustaining innumerable, often overlapping (and conflicting) human groups. Since talk is incessant among humans, I was cutting with the grain of actual everyday human experience, and could hope to understand the shape of human history as a whole by attending to the communication nets created by speech and to the ever-changing kinds of information circulating through them. More and more *The Rise of the West* began to seem archaic and inadequately conceived. I was exhilarated on the one hand, feeling like Moses on Mt. Pisgah, glimpsing the Promised

Land of intelligible world history from afar. And even though our house in Colebrook lies at the foot of another Mt. Pisgah, I knew full well that I was too old ever to write such a history on the scale and with the sort of up-to-date scholarship required.

This was my state of mind when my son, John Robert McNeill, by then a professor of history at Georgetown University, invited me to collaborate with him in writing "a very short history of the whole wide world," as we referred to the project at first. He had been teaching African history, among other subjects, and felt his students needed a way to situate what they were about to study within a world frame. Years before, my unhappy effort at collaboration with Frank Smothers had persuaded me to paddle my own canoe when it came to writing; but my son's proposal was attractive, and I was flattered to be invited. Moreover I had spare time with no other writing project in mind, so agreed to take on the first half of the book, and started work in 1997. I made a considerable effort to read anew in preparation for this task. The Yale History Department generously made me a visiting scholar, and this status allowed me to withdraw books from the library and keep them at home for weeks at a time. As a result, I could more or less reproduce the method of composition I had relied on when writing *The Rise of the West*, taking very few notes and composing the (deliberately few) footnotes with the cited source open before my eyes.

My son was then still finishing his own magnum opus, *Something New Under the Sun: An Environmental History of the Twentieth-Century World*,[17] so I finished a draft of my five chapters before he got round to starting his. That allowed him to read and react to my draft; and, as it turned out, we had plenty to argue about. He was intent on escaping from traditional Eurocentrism and wanted to address the Eurasian-African scene as a whole rather than dividing it among separate civilizations and, as he said, making the story of humankind into a horse race between rival civilized centers, as he thought I was still doing. Influenced by Wallerstein and Andre Gunder Frank, I had come round to the view that within Eurasia-Africa, transcivilizational connections did indeed constitute a "world system," and felt that my draft chapters said so. But of course Eurasia was not the world; another world system surely existed in the Americas and perhaps also within Oceania and Australia before European navigation inaugurated global transoceanic contacts. The term *world system* therefore was clumsy and obviously inadequate and, for me, was also marred by the quasi-Marxist emphasis on exploitation that Wallerstein and Gunder Frank had infused into it.

Resolution came abruptly one afternoon in the airport at Austin, Texas, where, in February 2000, my son and I had attended a conference on how to teach world history. Discussing our book while waiting for our homeward flights, he suddenly blurted out "the human web," short for web of communication. This echo of the World Wide Web, as commonly applied to contemporary electronic communication, was so powerful and apt that we both agreed at once that this was the term to use as the organizing concept for our book. It took further discussion before we agreed on exactly how to modify the term *web* in applying it to different ages and different patterns of society; but we achieved agreement within a few months, and I then had to revise all I had written to employ our chosen terminology. He meanwhile worked on his chapters, and I had my turn to criticize and make suggestions for revision as they came from his computer.

In addition, Steve Forman, an editor at W. W. Norton, went over our text, changing some words and sentences to make them simpler.

I was not accustomed to allowing my prose to be tampered with by editors, and vetoed some of his changes, but had to admit that many of them were for the better. My son also rewrote short passages in my chapters, so when *The Human Web: A Bird's-Eye View of World History* (2003)[18] finally came out, reading the published text became a strange experience. Throughout the first half of the book, I could savor passages of familiar discourse only to be surprised, here and there, but over and over, by a few alien words and sentences. Yet overall the end result was simpler and clearer than my version had been. In short, our book was indeed a joint product, and we both feel pleased and proud of our collaboration.

The publisher did not advertise *The Human Web*, so far as I know, and it was not widely reviewed in newspapers and literary journals, save for a sympathetic but not very incisive review in the *New York Review of Books*, written by Jonathan Spence, Yale's distinguished historian of early modern China. Nonetheless, I have some hope that the concept of the human web will catch on and that our central notion of patterns of communication, changing with improvements in transport and information storage and retrieval, will strike other historians as a better way to understand the human past than the explanations allowed by older schemes, whether multiple independent civilizations with Spengler and Toynbee; ancient, medieval, modern with humanists of the fifteenth century; stone, bronze, and iron ages with nineteenth-century archaeologists; or slave, serf, and hired labor with Marx.

Overall, *The Human Web* offers a more incisive and better balanced account of the civilizing process than has previously been available, and I consider it to be a fitting climax to my effort at understanding human history as a whole that dawned on me in my undergraduate days, widened in scope when I first read Toynbee at

Cornell in 1940, and achieved its initial scholarly formulation in 1963 with *The Rise of the West.* Forty years later, my son and I concocted a revised, corrected, and condensed version of the human story. Others will decide what to make of it; but my life's ambition is now accomplished to the best of my ability and to my own satisfaction.

Such smugness invites mockery, perhaps envy. But in old age, as my powers weaken, it is what I feel. Perhaps it would be wiser to keep such sentiments to myself, but as this memoir makes clear, my intellectual ambitions were never modest, and in old age I remain as eager to understand everything as when I was young. The difference is that I now know a good deal more and believe I have recognized at long last the key to humanity's extraordinary success in the balance of nature. In a nutshell, cooperation, sustained by incessant verbal communication, provoked distress whenever experience disappointed expectation. That, in turn, generated deliberate efforts to repair all the gaps between conscious purposes and actual processes, a sure and certain recipe for provoking new kinds of behavior. As a result, once language came fully on stream, perhaps only about forty thousand years ago, human groups began to transform the world around them in more and more far-reaching ways.

As always, the future remains uncertain, but the human past is indeed amazing and we are now able to see it whole, as was not yet the case in my youth. More generally, so conceived, our history as a species has become part of a new, evolutionary worldview, uniting physical, biological, and human reality into a single, ever-changing whole. This is the central intellectual accomplishment of the twentieth century, and I am pleased to think I played a small but significant part in constructing it.

Others continue to work along parallel lines. Study of world history has indeed begun to spread and, in the United States, recently displaced Western Civ as the principal supplement to U.S. national history to which high school students are exposed. Since 1990, the *Journal of World History* has been able to publish a long series of significant scholarly articles; and *World History Connected*, a new electronic journal designed to spread best practice among high school and college teachers of world history, made a promising debut in 2003.

Among a galaxy of practicing world historians, the person who most impresses me is David Christian, with whom I have corresponded for some time. His major book, *Maps of Time*, appeared in February 2004. It begins with the big bang and surveys the entire evolutionary story as cosmologists, physicists, geologists, biologists, archaeologists, and historians have been able to put it together. Thus *Maps of Time* enormously expands and complements our parallel but less inclusive effort. Christian's book, if it attracts appropriate attention, will count in future as a landmark synthesis, offering a far more complete account of the newly glimpsed evolutionary reality with which our book dealt only in part. My son and I, in short, are like John the Baptist, prefiguring a greater revelation coming from the hand and mind of David Christian.

*   *   *   *   *

In recent years, I have ceased traveling to conferences and stopped giving lectures, owing to my own debilities and my wife's ill health. Blurring eyesight also prevents reading as much as I used to. What remains is the pleasure of observing how rapidly my grandchildren become more and more mature human beings. Their expanding capabilities balance my own memories of past pleasures, achievements, and failures, some of which are here recorded.

It seems best to close with two superficially contradictory observations. First to say, as I did before when summarizing my military career, how my entire life has been unusually and quite fortuitously lucky. I can, for example, think of moments when I narrowly escaped sudden death. The penicillin that cured my pneumonia in 1951, for example, perhaps saved my life; the car that knocked me down on the Midway one icy night in the 1930s would surely have killed me if it had been traveling faster; and once I fell asleep and went off the road while driving between Chicago and Connecticut and might have killed myself and my elder son, but, as it happened, we both escaped unharmed. Everyone perhaps meets similarly close calls, but how incomplete my life would have been if I had died on any of the above occasions!

And how lucky I was to enjoy good health down almost to the present; how fortunate to have such parents; how privileged in my situation at the University of Chicago, with bright and ambitious students to learn from, and with colleagues who tolerated and sometimes even respected my intellectual ambitions. Last but not least, how blessed I was by a wife and children, who cheerfully put up with me and let me do my professional work with quiet mind. Few persons are so fortunate; yet without such support and without such institutions as the libraries I used, and the publishers who printed my books, my career as a historian would be inconceivable.

Yet there is something to what might be called un-Calvinistic, i.e., human rather than divine, predestination. Searching for photographs for this volume I ran across two long-forgotten verses that my father wrote on the occasion of my birth and pasted into my baby book. Here they are:

Prophecy for my Son

You come while still the deep skies lower
With strifes that make the people free:
Your drowsy eyes shall, in their hour
View wonders we may never see:
Your tender hands shall grasp with power
New keys to the old mystery!

Prayer for my Son

God shield you not from pain
But from unworthiness.
God send you hard-won joy for gain
And honor for success.

As this memoir attests, I did in fact strive to grasp "keys to the old mystery" more pertinaciously than most, and attained more than my share of "hard-won joy" as well.

Yet no one makes a self. I am, like everyone else, a creature of the web of communication that enveloped me from birth. My parents' high expectations were part of the web, in which, like everyone else, I participated from infancy. That will always be so while human society persists. But pressure to live up to my parents' expectations, combined with a large dose of personal pride and ambition, propelled me to read, read, read, and scribble, scribble, scribble. Through no choice of my own, therefore, my books and other writings add up to a larger and perhaps more enduring smudge within the human web than the transitory traces most persons leave in their wake. In that respect, too, I am surely and surprisingly, but not fortuitously, lucky.

Notes

1. From Childhood to World War II

1. This may be paraphrased as follows: God is the greatest and most perfect being we can conceive of. But it is greater and more perfect to exist than not to exist. Therefore God must exist.

2. That is, the teaching of St. Thomas Aquinas (d. 1274), officially accepted by the Roman Catholic Church.

3. William H. McNeill, Editorial, *Maroon*, 14 January 1938.

4. William H. McNeill, Editorial, *Maroon*, 27 May 1938.

5. Lynn White Jr., "Technology and Invention in the Middle Ages," *Speculum* (1940).

6. C. S. and C. S. Orwin, *The Open Fields* (London: Oxford University Press, 1938).

7. Arnold J. Toynbee, *A Study of History*, 3 vols. (London: Oxford University Press, 1934).

2. From Basic Training to *The Rise of the West*

1. William H. McNeill, *The Greek Dilemma; War and Aftermath* (Philadelphia: Lippincott, 1947).

2. William H. McNeill, "How the Potato Changed the World's History," *Social Research* 66 (Winter 1998): 67–83.

3. William H. McNeill, "Introduction of the Potato into Ireland," *Journal of Modern History* 21 (1949): 218–21.

4. Twentieth Century Fund, *Report on the Greeks* (New York: Twentieth Century Fund, 1948).

5. William H. McNeill, *The Handbook of Western Civilization* (Chicago: University of Chicago Press, 1949).

Notes

6. William H. McNeill, *America, Britain and Russia: Their Cooperation and Conflict, 1941–1946* (London: Oxford University Press, 1953).

7. G. von Grunebaum and W. Hartner, eds., *Klassicizmus und Kulturverfall* (Frankfurt am Main: Vittorio Klosterman, 1960).

8. Leften Stavrianos, *The Balkans since 1453* (New York: Rinehart, 1958).

9. William H. McNeill, *Arnold J. Toynbee: A Life* (New York: Oxford University Press, 1989).

10. William H. McNeill, *The Rise of the West: A History of the Human Community* (Chicago: University of Chicago Press, 1963).

11. William H. McNeill, "*The Rise of the West* after Twenty-five Years," *Journal of World History* 1 (1990): 1–21.

12. Marshall G. S. Hodgson, *The Venture of Islam* (Chicago: University of Chicago Press, 1974).

13. Marshall G. S. Hodgson, *Rethinking World History* (Cambridge: Cambridge University Press, 1993), pp. 92–93. These words come from a private letter Hodgson wrote in 1966.

14. McNeill, *The Rise of the West*, pp. 806–7.

3. From *The Rise of the West* to *Plagues and Peoples*

1. Carl Sagan, ed., *Communicating with Extra-Terrestrial Intelligence* (CETI), (Cambridge, MA: MIT Press, 1973), p. 346.

2. William H. McNeill, *A World History* (New York: Oxford University Press, 1967).

3. William H. McNeill, ed., *Readings in World History*, 9 vols. (New York: Oxford University Press, 1968–73).

4. William H. McNeill, *The Ecumene: Story of Humanity* (New York: Harpers, 1973).

5. William H. McNeill, *A History of the Human Community* (Englewood Cliffs, NJ: Prentice Hall, 1986).

6. William H. McNeill, *Past and Future* (Chicago: University of Chicago Press, 1954).

7. William H. McNeill, *Europe's Steppe Frontier, 1500–1800* (Chicago: University of Chicago Press, 1964).

8. William H. McNeill, *Venice: The Hinge of Europe, 1081–1797* (Chicago: University of Chicago Press, 1974).

9. William H. McNeill, *The Shape of European History* (New York: Oxford University Press, 1974).

10. Roger Mols, *Introduction à la démographie historique des villes d'Europe du XIVe au XVIIIe siècle*, 3 vols. (Gambloux: Duculot, 1954–56).

11. William H. McNeill, *Greece: American Aid in Action* (New York: The Twentieth Century Fund, 1957).

12. William H. McNeill, "Dilemmas of Modernization in Greece," *Balkan Studies* 8, no. 2: 305–16.

13. William H. McNeill, *The Metamorphosis of Greece since World War II* (Chicago: University of Chicago Press, 1978).

14. William H. McNeill, *Plagues and Peoples* (New York: Doubleday, 1976).

15. Alfred Crosby, *The Columbian Exchange: Biological and Cultural Consequences of 1492* (Westport, CT: Greenwood Press, 1972).

4. From *Plagues and Peoples* to Retirement

1. Michael Kammen, ed., *The Past Before Us: Contemporary Historical Writing in the United States* (Ithaca, NY: Cornell University Press, 1980).

2. Kammen, *Past*, p. 97.

3. Ibid., p. 112.

4. Francis Cornford, *Thucydides Mythistoricus* (London: Edward Arnold, 1907).

5. William H. McNeill, "Herodotus and Thucydides: A Consideration of the Structure of Their Histories" (master's thesis, University of Chicago, 1939), p. 90.

6. I published this essay in book form as *Mythistory and Other Essays* (Chicago: University of Chicago Press, 1986) and it also appeared as is customary in the *American Historical Review* 91 (March 1986).

7. Uno Svedin and Britt Aniansson, eds., *Surprising Futures* (Stockholm: Swedish Council for Planning and Coordination of Research, 1987), p. 51.

8. Neils Steensgaard, *The Asian Trade Revolution of the Seventeenth Century* (Chicago: University of Chicago Press, 1974).

9. Richard W. Bulliet, *The Camel and the Wheel* (New York: Columbia University Press, 1975).

10. William H. McNeill, "The Eccentricity of Wheels," *American Historical Review* 92 (Dec. 1987): 1111–26.

11. William H. McNeill, review of Immanuel Wallerstein, *The Modern World System: Capitalist Agriculture and the European World Economy in the 16th Century, Vol. 1* (New York: Academic Press, 1974), in *Societas* 6 (1976): 1, 39–40.

12. William H. McNeill, "The Rise of the West as a Long-Term Process," in *Mythistory and Other Essays* (Chicago: University of Chicago Press, 1986), pp. 43–67.

Notes

13. Johan Goudsblom, *Fire and Civilization* (London: Allen Lane, Penguin Press, 1992).

14. Joseph Needham, *Science and Civilization in China* (Cambridge: Cambridge University Press, 1954 and following).

15. William H. McNeill and Ruth S. Adams, eds., *Human Migration: Patterns and Policies* (Bloomington, IN: Indiana University Press, 1978).

16. William H. McNeill, "Human Migration: A Historical Overview," in McNeill and Adams, *Human Migration*, pp. 3–19.

17. William H. McNeill, "Human Migration in Historical Perspective," *Population and Development Review* 10 (1984): 1–19; also published in William Alonso, ed., *Population in an Interacting World* (Cambridge, MA: Harvard University Press, 1987), pp.15–35.

18. William H. McNeill, "On National Frontiers: Ethnic Homogeneity and Pluralism," in *Small Comforts for Hard Times*, ed. Michael Mooney and Florian Stuber (New York: Columbia University Press, 1977), pp. 207–19.

19. William H. McNeill, "The Conservation of Catastrophe," *Daedalus* 48 (Winter 1989): 1–15; Francis X. Sutton, ed., *A World to Make* (New Brunswick, NJ: Transaction Publishers, 1990), pp. 1–15; William H. McNeill, *The Global Condition* (Princeton, NJ: Princeton University Press, 1992), pp. 135–49.

20. William H. McNeill, *The Human Condition: An Ecological and Historical View* (Princeton: Princeton University Press, 1980).

21. William H. McNeill, *The Great Frontier: Freedom and Hierarchy in Modern Times* (Princeton: Princeton University Press, 1982).

22. William H. McNeill, *Polyethnicity and National Unity in World History* (Toronto: University of Toronto Press, 1986).

23. McNeill, *Frontier*, p. 31.

24. Walter Prescott Webb, *The Great Frontier* (Austin, TX: Texas University Press, 1964).

25. William H. McNeill, "The American War of Independence in World Perspective," in *Reconsiderations on the Revolutionary War*, ed. Don Higginbotham (Westport, CT: Greenwood Press, 1978), pp. 3–13.

26. William H. McNeill, "The Care and Repair of Public Myths," *Foreign Affairs* (Fall 1982): 1–13.

27. William H. McNeill, *The Pursuit of Power: Technology, Armed Force and Society since A.D. 1000* (Chicago: University of Chicago Press, 1982).

28. Robert Hartwell, "Markets, Technology and the Structure of Enterprise in the Development of the Eleventh-Century Chinese Iron and Steel Industry," *Journal of Economic History* 20 (1966): 29–58; Robert Hartwell, "A Cycle of Economic Change in Imperial China: Coal and Iron in Northeast

Notes
===

China, 750–1350," *Journal of Economic and Social History of the Orient* 10 (1967): 103–59; Robert Hartwell, "Financial Expertise, Examinations and the Formulation of Economic Policy in Northern Sung China," *Journal of Asian Studies* 30 (1971): 281–314.

29. Mark Elvin, *The Pattern of the Chinese Past* (Stanford, CA: Stanford University Press, 1973).

30. Yoshinobu Shiba, *Commerce and Society in Sung China* (Ann Arbor, MI: University of Michigan Press, 1970).

5. Retirement in Colebrook

1. Kirkpatrick Sale, *The Conquest of Paradise: Christopher Columbus and the Columbian Legacy* (New York: Plume, 1990).

2. William H. McNeill, "*The Rise of the West* after Twenty-five Years," *Journal of World History* 1 (Spring 1990): 1–23.

3. William H. McNeill, *Population and Politics since 1750* (Charlottesville, VA: University of Virginia Press, 1990), Preface.

4. William H. McNeill, review of Ernest Gellner, *Plow, Sword and Book: The Structure of Human History* (Chicago: University of Chicago Press, 1989), in *History and Theory* 29 (1990): 234–40.

5. William H. McNeill, "Fundamentalism and the World of the 1990s," in *Fundamentalism and Society: Reclaiming the Sciences, the Family and Education,* ed. Martin E. Marty and R. Scott Appleby (Chicago: University of Chicago Press, 1993), pp. 558–73.

6. William H. McNeill, *The Disruption of Traditional Forms of Nurture, Essay and Discussion* (Amsterdam: Het Spinhuis, 1998).

7. William H. McNeill, "Introductory Historical Commentary," in *The Fall of Great Powers: Peace, Stability and Legitimacy,* ed. Geir Lundestad (New York: Oxford University Press, 1994), pp. 3–23.

8. Praemium Erasmianum Foundation, *Praemium Erasmianum, 1958–1983* (Amsterdam: Stichtung Praemium Erasmianum, 1983), Foreword.

9. Subsequently published with minor changes as "History and the Scientific World View," *History and Theory* 37 (1998): 1–13.

10. William H. McNeill, "A Short History of Humanity," *New York Review of Books* 29 (June 2000): 9–11.

11. William H. McNeill, "Passing Strange: The Convergence of Evolutionary Science with Scientific History," *History and Theory* 40 (2001): 1–15.

12. McNeill, *Toynbee.*

13. William H. McNeill, *Hutchins' University: A Memoir of the University of Chicago, 1929–1959* (Chicago: University of Chicago Press, 1991).

Notes

14. William H. McNeill, *Colebrook: An Historical Sketch* (Colebrook: Colebrook Historical Society, 1996).

15. William H. McNeill, *Grandfather Stories* (Privately printed, 1996).

16. William H. McNeill, *Keeping Together in Time: Dance and Drill in Human History* (Cambridge, MA: Harvard University Press, 1995).

17. John Robert McNeill, *Something New Under the Sun: An Environmental History of the Twentieth-Century World* (New York: W. W. Norton, 2000).

18. William H. McNeill and John Robert McNeill, *The Human Web: A Bird's-Eye View of World History* (New York: W. W. Norton, 2003).

William H. McNeill Publications

Note: Books are listed chronologically. Essays are grouped
under topical headings and alphabetized.

Books and Edited Volumes

1947   *The Greek Dilemma; War and Aftermath.* Philadelphia: Lippincott.

1948   *History Handbook of Western Civilization.* Chicago: University of
Chicago Press. (6th ed. published 1986.)

1948   *Report on the Greeks.* New York: Twentieth Century Fund.

1953   *America, Britain and Russia: Their Cooperation and Conflict, 1941–
1946.* London: Oxford University Press.

1954   *Past and Future.* Chicago: University of Chicago Press.

1957   *Greece: American Aid in Action, 1947–56.* New York: Twentieth Century Fund.

1963   *The Rise of the West: A History of the Human Community.* Chicago:
University of Chicago Press. (Rev. ed. published 1991.)

1964   *Europe's Steppe Frontier, 1500–1800.* Chicago: University of Chicago
Press.

1967   *A World History.* New York: Oxford University Press. (4th ed. published 1999.)

William H. McNeill Publications

1967 *The Contemporary World: 1914–Present.* Glenview, IL: Scott, Foresman. (Rev. ed. published 1975.)

1967 Acton, John Emerich Edward Dalberg, Baron. *Essays in the Liberal Interpretation of History: Selected Papers.* Edited by William H. McNeill. Chicago: University of Chicago Press.

1968–73 McNeill, William H., Jean W. Sedlar, and others, eds. *Readings in World History.* 10 vols. New York: Oxford University Press.

1970 McNeill, William H., Sir Herbert Butterfield and Cho Yun Hsu. *On Chinese and World History.* Hong Kong: Chinese University of Hong Kong.

1973 *The Ecumene: Story of Humanity.* New York: Harpers.

1973 McNeill, William H., and Marilyn Robinson Waldman, eds. *The Islamic World.* Chicago: University of Chicago Press. (2nd ed. published 1983.)

1974 *The Shape of European History.* New York: Oxford University Press.

1974 *Venice: The Hinge of Europe, 1081–1797.* Chicago: University of Chicago Press.

1976 *Plagues and Peoples.* Garden City, NY: Anchor Press. (Rev. ed. published 1989.)

1978 *The Metamorphosis of Greece since World War II.* Chicago: University of Chicago Press.

1978 McNeill, William H., and Ruth S. Adams, eds. *Human Migration: Patterns and Policies.* Bloomington, IN: Indiana University Press.

1980 *The Human Condition: An Ecological and Historical View.* Princeton, NJ: Princeton University Press.

1982 *The Pursuit of Power: Technology, Armed Force and Society since A.D. 1000.* Chicago: University of Chicago Press.

William H. McNeill Publications

1983   *The Great Frontier: Freedom and Hierarchy in Modern Times.* Princeton, NJ: Princeton University Press.

1986   *Mythistory and Other Essays.* Chicago: University of Chicago Press.

1986   *Polyethnicity and National Unity in World History.* Toronto: University of Toronto Press.

1986   *A History of the Human Community: Prehistory to the Present.* Englewood Cliffs, NJ: Prentice-Hall. (6th ed. published 1998.)

1989   *The Age of Gunpowder Empires, 1450–1800.* Washington, DC: American Historical Association.

1989   *Arnold J. Toynbee: A Life.* New York: Oxford University Press.

1990   *Population and Politics since 1750.* Charlottesville: University Press of Virginia.

1991   *Hutchins' University: A Memoir of the University of Chicago, 1929–1950.* Chicago: University of Chicago Press.

1992   *The Global Condition: Conquerors, Catastrophes, and Community.* Princeton, NJ: Princeton University Press.

1995   *Keeping Together in Time: Dance and Drill in Human History.* Cambridge, MA: Harvard University Press.

1998   *The Disruption of Traditional Forms of Nurture: Essay and Discussion.* Amsterdam: Het Spinhuis.

2003   McNeill, William H., and J. R. McNeill. *The Human Web: A Bird's-Eye View of World History.* New York: W. W. Norton.

2005   *The Pursuit of Truth: A Historian's Memoir.* Lexington, KY: University Press of Kentucky.

William H. McNeill Publications

Selected Essays and Book Reviews

Public Affairs

"The Care and Repair of Public Myth." *Foreign Affairs* 61 (1982): 1–13.

"Fundamentalism and the World of the 1990s." In *Fundamentalism and Society*, ed. Martin E. Marty and Scott Appleby, 553–73. Chicago: University of Chicago Press, 1993.

"Multiculturalism in History: An Imperative of Civilization." *Orbis*, fall 1999, 541–51.

"The Peasant Revolt of Our Times." In *Changing Perspectives on Man*, ed. Ben Rothblatt, 229–42. Chicago: University of Chicago Press, 1968.

"Winds of Change." In *Sea Change: American Foreign Policy in a World Transformed*, ed. Nicholas Rizopoulos, 163–203. New York: Center on Foreign Relations Press, 1998.

World History

"The Changing Shape of World History." *History and Theory* 34 (1995): 8–26.

"A Defense of World History." *Transactions of the Royal Historical Society*, 1982, 75–89.

"How to Think about World History." Preface in *The World System*, ed. Andre Gunder Frank and Barry Gills. London: Routledge, 1993.

"Organizing Concepts for World History." *Review: Fernand Braudel Center, SUNY* 10 (1986): 211–29.

"*The Rise of the West* after Twenty-five Years." *Journal of World History* 1 (1990): 1–12.

"World History and the Rise and Fall of the West," *Journal of World History* 9 (1998): 215–36.

William H. McNeill Publications

Social Theory

"The Biological Basis of Human History." *Perspectives in Biology and Medicine* 46 (2003): 371–82.

"Control and Catastrophe in Human Affairs." *Daedalus* 48 (1989): 1–12.

"History and the Scientific World View." *History and Theory* 37 (1998): 1–13.

"Mythistory, or Truth, Myth, History and Historians." *American Historical Review* 91 (1986): 1–10.

Historical Revisionism

"The American War of Independence in World Perspective." In *Reconsiderations on the Revolutionary War*, ed. Don Higginbotham, 3–13. Westport, CT: Greenwood Press, 1978.

"The Eccentricity of Wheels, or Eurasian Transportation in Historical Perspective." *American Historical Review* 92 (1987): 1111–26.

"European Expansion, Power and Warfare since 1500." In *Imperialism and War*, ed. J. A. DeMoor and H. L. Wesseling, 12–21. Leiden: E. J. Brill, 1989.

"How the Potato Changed World History." *Social Research* 66 (1998): 67–83.

"Infectious Alternatives: The Plague That Saved Jerusalem, 701 B.C." In *What If?*, ed. Robert Crowley, 1–12. New York: G. P. Putnam's Sons, 1999.

"Information and Transport Nets in World History." In *World System History*, ed. Robert Denemark, et al., 203–215. London: Routledge, 2000.

"Introductory Historical Commentary." In *The Fall of Great Powers: Peace, Stability, and Legitimacy*, ed. Geir Lundestad, 3–22. Oslo, Norway: Scandinavian University Press, 1994.

"Men, Machines and War." In *Men, Machines and War*, ed. Ronald Haycock and Keith Neilson, 1–20. Waterloo, Ontario: Wilfred Laurier University Press, 1988.

"On National Frontiers: Ethnic Homogeneity and Pluralism." In *Small Comforts for Hard Times*, ed. Michael Mooney and Florence Stuber, 207–19. New York: Columbia University Press, 1977.

Population and Migration

"Human Migration in Historical Perspective." *Population Development Review* 10 (1984): 1–18.

"The Repopulation of the Americas in Historical Perspective." *International Journal of Population Geography* 9 (2003): 83–91.

Universities and Learning

"Trends in Scholarship in the Social Sciences." In *Rededication to Scholarship*, ed. James K. Robinson, 35–45. Cincinnati: University of Cincinnati, 1980.

"The University and the History of Ideas." In *The Mission of the University*. Kingston, Ontario: Queen's University, n.d., 14–23.

Book Reviews and Appraisals of Individual Historians

"Basic Assumptions of Toynbee's *A Study of History*." In *The Intent of Toynbee's History: A Cooperative Appraisal*, ed. Edward Gargan. Chicago: Loyola University Press, 1961.

"A Cartesian Historian." Review of *The Struggle for Mastery in Europe, 1848–1918*, by A. J. P. Taylor. *World Politics* 8 (1955): 124–33.

"Fernand Braudel, Historian." *Journal of Modern History* 73 (2000): 233–46.

"Toynbee Revisited." In *Adventures with Britannia: Personalities, Politics and Culture in Britain*, ed. Wm. Roger Louis. London: I. B. Tauris, 1995.

William H. McNeill Publications

Review of *Chaos and Governance*, by Giovanni Arrighi and Beverly Silva. *Political Power and Social Theory* 13 (1999): 299–305.

Review of *The Conquest of Paradise: Christopher Columbus and the Columbian Legacy*, by Kirkpatrick Sale. *New York Times*, 7 October 1990, 28.

Review of *Geopolitics and Geoculture: Essays in the Changing World System*, by Immanuel Wallerstein. *Diplomatic History* 18 (1994): 269–76.

Review of *Guns, Germs, and Steel: The Fates of Human Societies*, by Jared Diamond. *New York Review of Books*, 15 May 1997, 48–50.

Review of *The Memory Palace of Matteo Ricci*, by Jonathan Spence. *Boston Sunday Globe*, 18 November 1984.

Review of *The Nature of History*, by Arthur Marwick, and *Comment on écrit l'histoire*, by Paul Veyne. *History and Theory* 11 (1977): 103–9.

Review of *Plough, Sword and Book*, by Ernest Gellner. *History and Theory* 19 (1990): 231–40.

Review of *The Wealth and Poverty of Nations*, by David Landes. *New York Review of Books*, 5 April 1988, 37–39.

Index

Adams, Ruth, 121
Adler, Mortimer, 7, 15, 16, 27, 113
Africa, 74, 77, 153–54
agriculture, 34–35, 120;
    mechanized, 144; in Ottoman
    empire, 98; potato cultivation,
    40; steppe frontier in eastern
    Europe, 96; *zadruga,* 42
AIDS epidemic, 103
Air Force Academy (Colorado),
    128, 138
Akbar (Mughal emperor), 71
Alfred, king of England, 5
*America, Britain and Russia: Their
    Cooperation and Conflict,
    1941–1946* (McNeill), 62, 94
American Academy of Arts and
    Sciences, 121
"American century," 61
American Historical Association
    (AHA), 78–79, 107–8, 110, 117
American Historical Review, 30, 107
"American War of Independence in
    World Perspective, The"
    (McNeill, lecture), 124–25
Americas, pre-Columbian, 74, 154
Amerindians, 61, 102, 124, 136;

Columbus quincentenary and,
    133, 134–35; culture traits
    borrowed by, 26
Anderson, Eugene, 10, 11
Anselm, Saint, 8, 10
anthropology/anthropologists, 22,
    26, 68, 113, 121, 139; cultural,
    23–24; Erasmus Prize and, 148;
    historians and, 99
Antonine Plagues, 101, 102, 114
Arabic language, 72
archaeologists, 155
architecture, 82, 97
Aristotelianism, 15, 16
Aristotle, 58, 73
Armenia/Armenians, 84, 89–91, 98,
    142, 146
Arnold J. Toynbee: A Life (McNeill),
    69, 148
art, 10, 27, 70, 79–81, 85
*Asian Trade Revolution of the
    Seventeenth Century, The*
    (Steensgaard), 118
astronomy, 13, 89–91
Athens, ancient, 20, 24, 31
Athens, modern, 49, 50, 51, 52–53,
    82

175

Index

Australia, 102, 114, 154
Austria/Austrians, 66, 81
axe, as technology, 35
Aztec empire, 101

Bachofer, Ludwig, 70
Bailyn, Bernard, 121–22
Balkans, 38, 52, 57, 60, 66, 98
Balkans since 1453, The (Stavrianos), 66
Balliol College, Oxford, 61, 117
Barnes, Harry Elmer, 41
Barra (Hebridean island), 81–83
Beadle, George, 64, 77
Beatles, the, 82
Beatrix, queen of the Netherlands, 148
Becker, Carl, 11, 22, 29, 36, 40–41, 54
Belgium, 29, 30, 33
Benedict, Ruth, 23
Bentley, Jerry, 138
Bible, 4, 15, 75
big bang, 120, 157
"Big History," 120
Billias, George, 123
Billington, James, 151
biology, 13, 32, 116, 135, 146, 156
Biraben, J. N., 102
Black Death, 102
Black history, 77
Bloch, Marc, 30, 34
Bloor Street Presbyterian Church (Toronto), 4
Bolshevik Revolution, 1, 22
Borah, Woodrow, 102
Boserup, Ester, 120
Bosniak Muslims, 98

Bradley Commission, 109
Braudel, Fernand, 71, 79
Brazil, 141, 142–43
Britain, 5, 24, 25, 34, 81–82, 108; Celtic fringe of, 55; Greek civil war and, 50, 51, 56; historians in, 102; Hong Kong colony and, 84–85, 86, 87; industrial revolution in, 139; military-industrial complex in, 127–28; World War I and, 117
British Columbia, Canada, 1, 3
Brown, Stuart, 120
Bruère, Richard, 27
Brunner, Heinrich, 30
Buber, Martin, 148
Bucharest, 107, 108
Bulgaria, 81
Bulliet, Richard W., 118
Burckhardt, Jacob, 147
Burke, Edmund, III, 72, 73
Bush, George W., 122
Butterfield, Herbert, 84
Byurakan Astro-Physical Observatory (Armenia), 91

Cairo, Egypt, 48
Cambridge University (England), 150
Camel and the Wheel, The (Bulliet), 118
Canada, 1, 2, 4, 124
capitalism, 14, 50, 118–19, 126–27
Caractères originaux de l'histoire rurale française, Les (Bloch), 30, 34
Carnegie Foundation, 66, 67

176

Index

Index

Index

Hartner, Willi, 66
Hartwell, Robert, 126
Hawaii, University of, 116, 126
Haydon, Harold, 80
Heavenly City of the Eighteenth-Century Philosophers (Becker), 22
Hellenistic philosophy, 16
Herodotus, 25, 28, 52, 111
"Herodotus and Thucydides: A Consideration of the Structure of Their Histories" (McNeill, M.A. thesis), 27–28
Heyduks, 96
Hindu civilization, 41, 115
historians: biases and, 96, 135; economic, 143; Europeanists, 110; intellectual respectability of, 59; interchanges between, 73; nineteenth-century, 6; scientific branches and, 157; speculation and, 122, 129–30
history, 2, 109; cyclical pattern of, 21, 22, 24, 39, 68; meaning in, 25; religion in, 11; specialties of, 77; writing of, 62–64
History and Theory (journal), 148
History of the Human Community, A (McNeill), 93, 129
Hodgson, Marshall G. S., 71–72, 73, 74, 136
Holbein, Hans, 147
Hong Kong, 84–89
Horton, Douglas, 8–9
Houser, Schuyler, 92
Howard, Sir Michael, 117
Hull, Cordell, 48

Human Condition, The: An Ecological and Historical View (McNeill), 122
"Human Migration: A Historical Overview" (McNeill), 121
Human Migration: Patterns and Policies (conference papers), 121
"Human Migration in Historical Perspective" (McNeill), 121–22
Human Nature and Conduct (Dewey), 14
Human Web, The: A Bird's-Eye View of World History (McNeill and McNeill), 73, 155
Hungarians, 108
Huron Street Public School (Toronto), 6
Hutchins, Robert Maynard (college president), 7, 9–10, 15, 16, 27; as debater, 21; diminished admiration for, 149; as exemplar of intellectual life, 31; ideal of liberal education, 58; intercollegiate football and, 20
Hutchins' University: A Memoir of the University of Chicago, 1929–1959 (McNeill), 148
Hyde Park United Church (Chicago), 8

imperialism, 25, 47
Inalcik, Halil, 114
India, 25, 71, 77, 115
Indiana, University of, 107, 121

Index

Indians, North American. *See* Amerindians

industrial revolution, 40, 75, 82

International Congress of Anthropological and Ethnological Sciences, 99

Introduction à la démographie historique des villes d'Europe du XIVe au XVIIIe siècle (Mols), 100

Iraq war (from 2003), 122

Ireland, 42, 54

Iriye, Mitsuko, 92

Islam, 38, 71, 136–37; Bosniak Muslims, 98; caravan trade in Asia and, 118; in Morocco, 139, 140

Italian Americans, 133

Italy/Italians, 97, 98

Japanese history, 77, 116

Jesus, 11

Jews, 38, 88, 90, 98, 142

John Carter Brown Library, 135

Jones, E. L., 120, 127

Journal of Modern History (JMH), 55, 78–79

Journal of World History, 70, 137, 138, 157

Jowett, Benjamin, 15

Judaism, 38

Kadlec, Susan, 120

Kaegi, Werner, 147

Kammen, Michael, 107

Kates, Robert W., 114, 115

Keeping Together in Time: Dance and Drill in Human History (McNeill), 149, 151

Keller, Frances Richardson, 110

Kennedy, Paul, 145

Kindelberger, Charles, 143

"Klassicizmus und Kulturverfall" conference (1956), 65

Kondratieff cycles, 119

Korean War, 94

Kroeber, Alfred, 23

Ladurie, Emmanuel Le Roy, 102

Lafayette, Marquis de, 64–65

Landes, David, 143

Lane, Nancy, 107

language, social role of, 139–40, 151, 156

Larrabee, Col. Sterling, 48–49

Larsen, J. A. O., 27

Latin America, 141

Latinos, 133

Laue, Theo von, 123

Laws, The (Plato), 31

Lee Knowles lectures on military history, 150

Lemisch, Jesse, 78

Lenin, Vladimir I., 1

Levi, Edward, 77, 81

Lévi-Strauss, Claude, 148

liberalism, 24–25, 125

Library of Congress, 139, 151

Link, Arthur, 108–9, 110

Linton, Ralph, 23

literature, 10, 58

Livy, 27

Luce, Henry, 61

Lundestad, Geir, 145

Index

Luther, Martin, 58
Luxembourg Institute for European and International Studies, 143
Lytle, Scott, 36

Macedonia, Yugoslav, 81
Maclean, Norman, 17, 72
McDougall, Walter, 120
McGill University, 2, 3, 12
McKeon, Richard, 5, 15–16, 27, 58, 59
McKeown, Thomas, 102
McNeill, Elizabeth Darbishire, 52–53, 81–82, 106
McNeill, Isabel, 4
McNeill, J. R., 73
McNeill, John, 82–83
McNeill, John Robert, 153
McNeill, William H.: birth, 1, 3; children of, 53, 58, 67, 82, 83, 105; at Cornell University, 29–43, 94; on faculty of U. of Chicago, 58–60, 62, 63; family of, 1–4, 29, 88, 105, 149, 158–59; marriage, 53; Ph.D dissertation, 21, 40, 54, 55, 58, 60, 139; as president of American Historical Association, 107–10; retirement, 92, 106–7, 131–32, 138; vacation trips, 81–83; in World War II, 45–53
MacVeagh, Lincoln, 48
Macy Foundation, 101
Madame Bovary (Flaubert), 10–11
Manchester, England, 82
Mandel Hall (U. of Chicago), 10, 21
Mao Zedong, 56

Maps of Time (Christian), 157
Marconi, Guglielmo, 90
Marino, John, 120
Marty, Martin, 140
Marx, Karl, 15, 22, 61, 155
Marxism, 14–15, 17, 67, 154
mathematics, 89–90, 140, 145, 146
Matisse, Henri, 11
Maurice of Orange, 150
Mead, Margaret, 23
medieval history, 1, 29, 125, 127
Mediterranée, La (Braudel), 71
Melby, Ernest, 21
Merida (Mexican city), 23
Metamorphosis of Greece since World War II, The (McNeill), 100
Mexico, 22, 77, 136
Middle Ages, 28, 40
Middle East, 34
migration, 121–22, 145
Mihailovich, Dragoljub, 48
military history, 125–29, 150
military life, in World War II, 45–53, 149–50
Milton, John, 75
Mind and Society, The (Pareto), 37
Modern Greek Studies Association, 113
Modern World System, The: Capitalist Agriculture and the European World Economy in the 16th Century (Wallerstein), 118–19
Mols, Roger, 100
Mommsen, Wolfgang, 145
Monnet, Jean, 148

183

Index

Montenegro, 81
Moore, Henry, 79–81, 148
Morocco, 139, 140
Morrison, Philip, 91
Moscow, 48, 97
Moscow Conference (1943), 48
Mosely, Philip, 38, 40, 41–42, 48
mouldboard cultivation, 34–35, 40, 42
Mozart, Wolfgang Amadeus, 17
multiculturalism, 88–89
Mumford, Lewis, 22
Muscovite empire, 96, 97
music, 10, 151
"Mythistory, or Truth, Myth, History and Historians" (McNeill, presidential address), 111–12
myths, 111, 125, 130

National Book Award, 70
National Council for History Education, 109
National Council for History Standards, 109
National Endowment for the Humanities (NEH), 132
Nationalists, Greek, 50
Nation magazine, 24
Nazis, 24, 25, 65, 119
Needham, Joseph, 120
"Nemesis: A Study of the Rise and Fall of Civilizations" (McNeill), 24, 26, 28, 39
Nemesis (ancient Greek notion), 24
Nervi, Pier Luigi, 80
Netherlands, 148, 150

New Harmony, Indiana, 121
New School for Social Research (New York), 55
New York Public Library, 42
New York Review of Books, 148, 155
New York Times Book Review, 69
New Zealand, 114
Nobel Prize, 148
Norman conquest, 5
Normandy, 34
Northwestern University, 66, 67
Norway, 145
note taking, 63
Nova Scotia, 2
Nove, Alec, 145
Nuclear Energy (Moore sculpture), 79–81

objectivity, as ideal, 111
Oceania, 154
Office of Strategic Services (OSS), 49
Office of War Information (OWI), 53
"On National Frontiers: Ethnic Homogeneity and Pluralism" (McNeill, lecture), 122
"On Truth" (McNeill, incomplete), 31, 35
Open Fields, The (Orwin and Orwin), 34
Oriental Institute, 71
Orthodox Christianity, 38, 98, 114
Orwin, C. S. and C. S., 34
Ottoman empire, 71, 77, 87, 96, 97
outlines, historical, 6–7
Owen, Robert, 121

Index

Oxford University, 102, 107, 116–17, 126, 152

Paoli, Pasquale, 124
Paradise Lost (Milton), 75
Pareto, Vilfredo, 37
Past and Future (McNeill), 94, 95
Past Before Us, The: Contemporary Historical Writing in the United States (Kammen, ed.), 107
Paul, Saint, 11
Pauly-Wissowa (Greco-Roman encyclopedia), 16
peasants, 82, 100, 127, 129, 144
Peru, 114
Peter the Great, 25
philosophy, 16, 27, 32, 73, 130
physics, 12, 13, 37, 146
Pidgeon, Rev. George, 4–5, 9
Pirenne, Henri, 34
Plagues and Peoples (McNeill), 77, 101–3, 116, 123, 128; Columbus quincentenary and, 132; rejected for publication, 102, 107, 152; speculations in, 122
Plato, 21, 26, 58, 73; political ambitions of, 31–32; *Republic*, 7, 15, 16, 27
Platonism, 31
Plow, Sword and Book: The Structure of Human History (Gellner), 33, 139
plows, 34–35
Poland/Poles, 38, 95, 98
political science, 13
polyethnicity, 122, 124, 145

Polyethnicity and National Unity in World History (McNeill), 122
Polynesians, 102
Population and Politics since 1750 (McNeill), 139
potato cultivation, 40, 42, 54–55
Presbyterianism, 2, 4, 10
Prince Edward Island, Canada, 2, 3, 88, 149
Protestantism, 1–2, 38, 124
Puerto Rico, 47, 48
Pugachev, Yemelyan Ivanovich, 124
Pursuit of Power, The: Technology, Armed Force and Society since A.D. 1000 (McNeill), 46, 117, 123, 125, 126–28, 149–50

Quebec, separatism in, 124
Quigley, Carroll, 125, 126

racial tensions: in Brazil, 142; in Chicago, 105
Radcliffe-Brown, A. R., 23
Raleigh, Walter, 55
Readings in World History (McNeill and Sedlar, eds.), 92
Reagan administration, 132
realpolitik, 25
reason, 11
Redfield, Robert, 22–23, 139
Reformation, Protestant, 1, 2, 38, 147
religion, 8–9, 11, 32, 98, 141, 145
Renaissance, 97, 98
"Renaissance and Reformation" (Troeltsch), 59
Report on the Greeks (McNeill and Smothers), 57

Index

Index

White, Lynn, Jr., 34
White Library (Cornell U.), 36
Whitenack, Jean, 68
Willem-Alexander of the
    Netherlands, Prince, 148
Williams, John, 132
Williams College, 136–37
Wilson, Woodrow, 109
Wissler, Clark, 26
Woodrow Wilson Center, 139
workers, unionized, 19
world history, 67, 71, 72, 73; in
    American schools, 93, 109,
    138, 157; Chinese history and,
    84; civilizational and national
    history compared to, 74;
    communication nets and, 152;
    opposition to, 131–32; Western
    Civilization course and, 92
World History, A (McNeill), 92, 93

World History Association (WHA),
    138
World History Connected
    (electronic journal), 157
World War I, 47, 66, 69, 125, 142;
    Britain in, 117; Germany in,
    25, 117, 127–28
World War II, 29, 42, 45–53, 125

Yale University, 151, 153, 155
Yalta Conference, 63
Yavlinski, Grigori, 141–42
"Year 1000 A.D., The, Being an
    Inquiry into the Rise of Towns
    in North Western Europe"
    (McNeill), 31, 33–34
Yoshinobu Shiba, 126
Yugoslavia, 48, 81

zadruga, South Slav, 42